ENDO

This is a mind-blowing book! It's a testimony to Michelle's obedience, God's faithfulness, and the shockingly blatant ignorance and prejudice that face so many women called to lead in the church. Read it and you'll know that God is on the move, calling and equipping women to help lead the church to a holy and hopeful future.

—*Danielle Strickland, author, international speaker, podcaster, and social justice advocate*

It is my privilege to recommend Felice's *Throw Another Pebble on the Pile*. The strength of the book is her honest recollection of the joys and challenges she has faced in church ministry. Felice has coined the perfect title. The obstacles women face in the church are like pebbles of different sizes, dropped one at a time, one small incident followed by another, which together become a large pile of rocks that injure the soul. My prayer is that Felice's memoir will play a part in leading the Church to treat everyone, male and female, as they should be treated as the creation of God.

—*Rev. Rick Love, PhD, pastor, and seminary professor*

My favourite aspect of Michelle's book is the way she's woven personal story into a robust discussion of practical insights, divine wisdom, and research findings on the devastating impact of patriarchy. She cleverly highlights both the covert and overt effects of a world that favours one gender above the other in direct contravention to the beautiful design of the Creator God. *Throw Another Pebble on the Pile* is timely, thoughtful, and sensitively written, offering the reader a pathway towards healing and understanding to a place where men and women can flourish together and be all they were created to be.

—*Tania Harris, PhD, pastor, practical theologian, author, broadcaster, and the Director of God Conversations*

Throw Another
Pebble on the Pile

Throw Another Pebble on the Pile

One Woman's Leadership Journey in the Church

MICHELLE FELICE

◆ FriesenPress

One Printers Way
Altona, MB R0G 0B0
Canada

www.friesenpress.com

Edited by Katie Heffring

Cover design by Alyssa Doucet

All Scripture references are from the New International Version of the Bible, unless otherwise indicated.

This work depicts actual events in the life of the author as truthfully as recollection permits and/or can be verified by research. The author has attempted to recreate conversations from her memories of them. All persons within are actual individuals; there are no composite characters. The names of some individuals have been changed to respect their privacy.

ISBN
978-1-03-832168-8 (Hardcover)
978-1-03-832167-1 (Paperback)
978-1-03-832169-5 (eBook)

1. RELIGION, CHRISTIAN CHURCH, LEADERSHIP

Distributed to the trade by The Ingram Book Company

*For every woman
with unmet aspirations
due to unfair obstacles*

TABLE OF CONTENTS

INTRODUCTION

Everyone in the hospital room stopped their quiet murmurings to hear what I would say. I sat at the bedside of an eighty-year-old man and he posed a question that made his three roommates and their guests stop talking. The sudden silence in the room was awkward and intimidating. I became acutely aware that everyone was waiting to hear my response. A surge of adrenaline released through my body as I mentally searched for a quick reply.

I was the only one in the room who knew that this man, a retired physician, had cancer that had spread throughout his body. His mental capacities were clouded. Moments before, no one else heard him ask me who I was, even though we had known each other for over twenty years. I reminded him that I was a pastor from his church, and he surprised me with his next declaration.

"There are women pastors now? I don't know if I agree with such a thing!"

I knew this was not the time to discuss theology or church governance because he wouldn't comprehend or have the patience to listen to any lengthy explanation. My response needed to be simple enough to satisfy him and appropriate enough for all the strangers in the room to hear.

"Yes, times have changed, and women can be pastors." I attempted to connect it to his sphere of experience. "I'm sure that when you were a young doctor, there weren't many female physicians, but now, no one thinks twice about that." The shock on his face.

He cried out, "There are women doctors now?"

The year was 2018.

I was relieved to hear chuckles from the neighbouring bed-sides, indicating to me that the other people in the room understood what was happening. His mind was back in a previous generation and not in the present day.

When I think of this encounter, it makes me smile. I remember the man who always made me laugh, literally right up until his final days. The irony of his assertion was that he had always supported me throughout the years. His statement was a product of the side effects of his sickness. But this anecdote is also a stark reminder for me of the systemic discrimination against women within the environment I had been a part of my whole life—the Christian church. Positive progress for equality is happening, but there's still a long way to go. And ingrained prejudices people have been taught since childhood are difficult to set aside.

As a female leader in the church, I have experienced many painful encounters. Each personal attack, each attempt to remind me that I didn't fully belong, and even every non-intentional condescending action has been like a pebble. Each one might be small and unable to do much damage on its own, but I would imagine a great pile of stones, and with every exclusionary or discriminatory wound, I would say to myself, "Throw another pebble on the pile." In my mind's eye, I would toss the small stone on the pile and then walk away. There! My pain is over there. I could compartmentalize it and move on. The pile held my emotional and spiritual suffering until the next pebble was added. The hurt was set aside, but it did not dissipate, and as the pile grew, so did my pain.

This is my story. It's not meant to hurt anyone or rail against the church. My hope is that my story shines a light on my experience of discrimination, creating conversations that will prevent unnecessary losses for others who are marginalized.

CHAPTER 1
Strange Questions

It was the strangest question I had ever received. I wasn't sure what to do, but walking away didn't seem to be the answer. Besides, he presented his inquiry to me so respectfully and genuinely.

"How can a woman be a pastor? Women menstruate!"

I was attending the Baptist General Conference of Canada's annual denominational meeting in 2017. Representatives from all the churches in our province were there. The itinerary always included inspirational talks, goal setting for the upcoming year, reconnecting with old friends, and a presentation of all the new pastors—and on that day, I was one of them.

Each of Canada's Baptist denominations holds a stance on women in church leadership. Some insist on male-only leadership; others allow women to work in any role. Our denomination fell in the middle. Each church could decide for itself if women could hold leadership positions. And each church was expected to respect the decisions of the others. So I wasn't surprised when I received a variety of responses to my introduction as a pastor on that day. Some in the crowd were pleased to meet me, expressing their delight that more women were finally being accepted in the field. Others had a difficult time containing their displeasure but practised the well-known adage that if you have nothing nice to say, don't say anything at all. They ignored me.

And then some were just simply polite. They didn't have anything personally against me, but they weren't so sure a woman should be a pastor. They took a neutral stance that was neither welcoming nor hostile.

At least the man with the question was honest and direct. He waited for my response, and I could tell he sincerely wanted me to explain. I asked him to elaborate, partly because his question was so bizarre, but I also needed some time to regain my composure. I felt like the actors on *Saturday Night Live* who are trying to suppress their laughter and deliver the script straight.

He repeated his question, adding some clarification: "How can a woman lead a church when she is prone to days of unpredictable mood swings? She can become emotional, even unstable."

I summoned up all the maturity I could muster. "Yes, many women do experience some emotional unpredictability due to hormonal changes, but it's something they must learn to manage in the workplace. But how is that any different than a man who struggles with his emotions? He too needs to learn how to put his game face on, come to work, and do his job."

The man looked at me with a confidence that indicated he was under no delusion of the correctness of his argument. As we continued chatting, an older woman approached, and I could tell she knew this man. She did not comment but became an observer of the conversation, and I had no idea on which side of the argument she resided. He eventually turned to her and said, "I've written an academic paper on this topic. Would you like to read it?"

"Nope!" And as she walked away, she said, "Maybe it's time you write a new paper!"

Thinking the conversation was done, I went to the lunch hall. But he found me. And for the next hour, I indulged his wish to talk theology and why a woman's biological functions did or did not pre-empt her from church leadership. The end of the lunch was not the end of the discussion in his mind. As he headed off to the afternoon sessions, he called out to me, "I look forward to continuing this conversation. I will call you at your church."

At our staff meeting the following week, I shared my encounter with my church colleagues to their great amusement. And I told our office manager that if that fellow calls for me, please tell him I didn't come to work that day—I stayed home because I was having my period.

Six months earlier, I had applied for the associate pastor job at the church where I'd been a member for twenty years. This position was not ground-breaking for a woman but certainly gave people's concepts of "norms" a nudge. This "second-in-command" role brought up questions and scenarios no one ever had to consider before. But it came at the perfect time for me, as I had just finished my master's degree at seminary.

I compiled my résumé and responses to the application questions. There were rounds of interviews from the search committee, the staff, and the church board. And I preached a candidating sermon. When it was finally decided that I was the leading contender for the position, the whole church was invited to a congregational Q&A session.

When the evening arrived, I was more excited than nervous because I enjoy talking about the things I'm passionate about. It was a good night, with many of the classic questions directed to me regarding vision, leadership style, and hopes for the church. And I didn't have to wait too long until the inevitable questions concerning my gender arose.

He presented his concern very courteously. A man asked me to explain why I thought it was acceptable for a woman to be in this position. For someone who has never been a part of "church world," this might seem like another strange question. But I knew exactly what he meant. Until recently, many churches have only allowed men to be in leadership positions. But ours wasn't like that.

Our denomination allowed each church its autonomy in deciding its practice regarding women in leadership. In our church, there were women on the board, our church's highest authority. Women had been invited into pastoral positions working with youth and families. And on a Sunday morning, women were active participants leading in various ways during our church services.

The people of our church had even voted on it. Many years earlier, our church's constitution had been changed to allow a woman to hold the position of associate pastor. But in the church's sixty-year history, the lead pastor and associate pastor roles had always been held by men. The potential for it to happen had never been a reality until that evening. I guess that words on a piece of paper presented a beautiful picture of equality, but their weight seemed fragile in light of present circumstances. I didn't mind his question, though. He was honest with his feelings and spoke to me directly about what was unsettling him. He seemed satisfied with my response, and it was good that he gave voice to the unsaid concerns of others in the room.

It's generally understood that most of communication is non-verbal, so the person who "spoke" the loudest that night *to me* was a man in the back row. No one else would have noticed, but I "heard" him. Prior to that evening, I already knew that he didn't support women in church leadership. He sat the entire evening with his arms crossed and his lips pursed. I knew that this evening was pivotal for positive change, but the troubled look on his face told me that he thought it was a change in the wrong direction. As the evening's Q&A proceeded, I told myself not to look at him. Like a comic who mustn't be bothered by the one person not laughing, or the lecturer ignoring the student who is obviously on social media rather than listening, I had to focus on the rest of the room that was engaging with me positively.

The church members voted, and I was affirmed for the role. In my new job, I would work closely with the lead pastor and cover for him in his absences. The unspoken questions that evening were, "What will occur if something happens to the lead pastor? Does that mean she's in charge?" But at that moment, the general goodwill of the people and my past-proven competency were enough to dismiss hypothetical situations.

Some people were assured that this arrangement was acceptable because there was still a man "covering" me, a male in charge. The idea was that, yes, I was being put in a position of authority, but there was still a man in higher authority above me. He would be responsible for my teaching, my mistakes, and any decisions I made. Even though I was given incredible liberty to work and teach as I wished, somehow none of my efforts were valid on their own—because they were all subject to male approval.

In that moment, I accepted all that as nonsense. At fifty years old, I would take full responsibility for both my accomplishments and my mistakes. What was meant to be reassuring for others was incredibly condescending to me. But I didn't push back on these assertions; they were what enabled me to take on the role I had been working toward for many years. If a few others needed that ideology to make them feel comfortable, that was their concern. It was the price I had to pay to do the job, and besides... they'll change their minds eventually, won't they?

Interestingly enough, the man-in-the-back-row's quiet dissent was never a problem for me beyond that day. It was others in the room who expressed their support for me on that night who I never would have imagined would eventually cause me so much grief.

CHAPTER 2
Demon Eyes

Now that I was on staff at the church, it meant I would do more preaching. I had already been presenting the occasional Sunday message before my hiring. I'd started a few years earlier when I first became an elder, a board member who is responsible for church governance and spiritual leadership. When I was being interviewed for the role of elder, the lead pastor, Chris, surprised me by inquiring if I would like to preach occasionally. None of the other board members did this. I was instantly intrigued but daunted. But the fear of speaking in front of a crowd was balanced with the thrill of the opportunity. I asked for six weeks to prepare, as I didn't know how anyone could put together a talk in just one week. But now, as a staff pastor, things would be a little different. My preaching rotation would increase from once every few months to once every month.

Chris heard that a large local church was hosting a preaching conference, and he suggested we attend together. I registered online but a week later was surprised to receive a phone call from the office administrator of the hosting church.

"Hello, I see that you have submitted a registration for our conference, but I was wondering if you have mistakenly listed your name instead of your pastor's."

"No, it's correct. The registration is for me."

He hesitated for a moment before continuing. "I see…except for this preaching conference is for those who are in church leadership and who also preach regularly."

It didn't take long for me to realize what was happening. But I also knew he was just the messenger, not the person who made the rules, so I had some compassion for him as he stumbled over his words. But he was going to have to say it; I wasn't going to do it for him.

I feigned ignorance and kept my tone sweet. "Yes, I fulfill all the requirements for attendance."

Silence.

He had no choice but to continue. "I'm very sorry, but this conference is only for men."

My head was reeling. I couldn't believe he said those words. "There's no indication of that on your website," was the only thing I could think to say at that moment.

"Well, I guess we're going to have to fix that," was his only reply.

I held back the anger that was welling up in me and asserted that I was going to need my money back. He assured me that I would be refunded, but it never happened, requiring me to call a second time after the conference. I was barred from an event that I was entirely qualified to attend simply because of my gender. There's no way they were going to exclude me and keep my money.

Preaching is only one part of being a pastor, but it is the element that brings the most praise or critique for the person in that role. There's the challenge of putting something concise, educational, and inspiring together. Then there's the, shall I say, terror of speaking in front of a few hundred people. But there's also something else, the thing that every female preacher can relate to. The weight of the moment.

When a man preaches for the first time, he only needs to do an adequate job, and everyone is proud of him. *Well done for your first time. You'll only get better from here.* He's given encouragement and grace as he begins to stretch in those preaching shoes. His starting point is where it should be—at the start.

But as a woman, if I only did an adequate job, I could already hear the post-service lunchtime conversation. *This is why we don't have women preachers.* I knew that my first sermon didn't need to be excellent, but it had to be better than average. I worked diligently on my first Sunday message, reading it out loud to make sure it flowed smoothly and practising it on the platform to familiarize myself with the blinding glare of the stage lights. I wanted to be as prepared as possible, because I knew that once I stepped onto that stage and before my mouth even opened, some people would already be biased against me. In some people's minds, a woman preaching was neither normal nor acceptable. And this wasn't just about me. Even if it wasn't true, I felt the weight of representing all women. Fortunately, my first presentation was received well, and it was the beginning of the congregation's acceptance of me in the role of teacher.

Like most skills, public speaking needs to be practised to gain proficiency. Passion will only get you so far. My seminary experience taught me how to put a talk together, but I knew that poor presentation could get in the way of delivering a message. So YouTube became my friend as I searched for videos on public speaking, and I started to appreciate how much my body language could help or hinder my sermons.

As I became more comfortable on the stage, I learned to use my arms with open expressions to appear more welcoming. I moved away from standing behind the pulpit, because at five foot one, most people could only see me from the chest up, creating a bobblehead effect. I controlled my laughter to never present as a giggle. I learned not to touch my hair, even when it fell into my eyes or got caught in my mic, fearing that this feminized action would be too distracting. I adapted my way of speaking and moving around the stage so that it would be acceptable to those in the room.

I soon discovered that there was another challenge for women that most men don't need to consider—the register of their voice. A woman's voice can lilt up at the end of a sentence, making it difficult for the listener to follow. Also, the higher pitch of a woman's voice is harder to hear in a large room and presents less authoritative than a man's. Unfortunately, we have been conditioned to accept that a high voice doesn't have the same gravitas or believability as a low voice.

In *Invisible Women: Data Bias in a World Designed for Men*, Caroline Criado Perez shares the ways the world's default setting for almost everything is male. She tells the story of a woman and her new car. The woman was frustrated that her car's voice-command system didn't acknowledge her verbal commands but responded to the person in her passenger seat—her husband. When she called the manufacturer, the only help she received was the advice to lower her voice when speaking to her car. It worked. The vehicle was simply not programmed to respond to a woman's voice.[1]

For women, there's another element while preaching that seems superficial to consider, but it's important. What to wear. Men can wear almost anything, from suits to ripped jeans and unpressed T-shirts. But I didn't want anything I wore to be a hindrance to the message being presented; being a woman was distraction enough. For my first sermon, I decided upon a mono-chromatic outfit of dark dress pants and a blouse. Bra straps were pinned in place because no one could hear from God at the appearance of a bra strap. Low pumps finished up the attire, giving me a professional but certainly not-seductive-in-any-way

....

1   Caroline Criado Perez, *Invisible Women: Data Bias in a World Designed for Men* (New York, NY: Abrams Press, 2019), 162.

look. In fact, the clothes I wore for my debut preach were so boring, I decided to liven up my look with some dangly earrings.

As I walked up on the stage to deliver my first sermon, my nerves were on high alert. I attempted to appear at ease while presenting my message without looking at my notes too much. Things seemed to be going smoothly. But what was that noise? *Tic, tic, tic.* I knew the whole room could hear it. I was wearing a head mic, the kind that rock stars wear so that their hands are free, and it didn't take me long to realize that my dangly earrings were hitting the mic each time I moved my head. Yikes, so much for feeling at ease on stage. I then had the awkward challenge of keeping my head completely still for the rest of the message while trying to appear relaxed. After that, stud earrings became the jewellery of choice for every sermon.

After my first few Sundays in my new uniform, a young man made an interesting comment to me. He appreciated what I shared that morning and mentioned that I looked very professional up on the stage. He offhandedly said, "It's not like you'd ever wear a dress up there." I'm sure he didn't mean anything negative by it, but it got me thinking. *Why can't I wear a dress? Why can't I dress like a woman if that's what I choose?* I immediately headed to the mall to find the perfect dress. Nothing was going to prevent me from wearing one the next time I preached. The challenge was on!

It's a frustrating process to find the right dress for such a task. It would be lovely to wear a shift dress, one that draped down to my knees revealing very little of my body beneath but offering me a lovely balance of comfort and femininity. But no, there's always the mic pack to consider. Guys can always shove it in their pockets, but women need an outfit with a waistband. (One preaching friend shared with me that in an unprepared moment, she had to put the pack in her underwear.) Eventually, I settled on the combination of a modest pencil skirt and blouse.

It shouldn't be about the apparel; it's about the message. But for women, the wrong apparel gets in the way of the message. Seeing a woman preach was not a norm for the people in my church, so I put energy into how I dressed. Present taller. Don't dress too femininely. Speak like a man. Avoid overtly feminine gestures. Then people will be able to "hear" you.

Sometimes it felt like I put too much energy into presenting the message like one of the men. But as the months passed, I started to care less about those details. Lowering my voice and making my presence larger on stage started to become second nature, and once I realized I was able to command the attention of the room with eye contact and using my voice effectively, I relaxed and enjoyed myself more. I was finally able to focus on those I was speaking to rather than on myself.

It wasn't until a few years later when one of the elders requested a meeting with me that I realized there were new things to be concerned about when I presented the Sunday morning message.

A board member called and said he needed to talk to me. His tone and directness told me something serious was on his agenda. The next day as I waited for him in my office, I was not worried because I could not imagine any potential problem. When he arrived, he immediately proceeded to tell me what was troubling him.

"A couple of church members have shared that when you preach on Sunday mornings, you are shooting out demonic looks at them." Not just snarky looks. Or sidewise eyes. No, surely the devil was in me, and he was looking at them through me.

I started to laugh.

"You need to stop laughing. This isn't funny."

But I couldn't stop laughing because, yes, it was funny! It was bizarre and unbelievable. And that's what made it so comical. He continued to insist that this wasn't a laughing matter, so I pulled myself together so we could have a serious conversation. I knew intuitively that the root of this complaint was based on my gender. I guess I should have felt relieved that the people who wanted to discredit me because I was a woman couldn't find concerns with my competencies or character. They had to go with crazy accusations.

The board member's insistence that the situation was not funny was his concern regarding the lengths some people would go to get what they wanted. He came to me not because he felt there was any validity to these accusations, but because he was concerned with people's tactics. And that wasn't funny—I agreed.

"How did our church get to this point?" he lamented.

Yes, how? How did we get to this point?

CHAPTER 3

Unlikely Career Change

In 2004, fifteen years before those crazy accusations, I applied for a job at my church. My friends were surprised and didn't understand why. But I knew. The calling I had felt as a child had reemerged. I had always felt that my vocation was to work for God but never really knew what that would look like.

I grew up on Vancouver Island, off the west coast of Canada. Our family lived in a small rural community just outside the town of Courtenay, and our home backed onto the Salish Sea and looked over to the mountains of British Columbia's mainland. Vancouver Island's population is often mistaken by visitors. Once, when my husband and I were on a cruise to Alaska, an Australian couple pointed toward its coastline and said, "We hear that there are people who live on that island."

"Yes," I replied, "over 800,000."

As a child, I was competitive. I excelled at school, in my piano lessons, and was even the chess champion of my city for grades five, six, and seven. In grade eight, I and all the other children from our small community were bussed into Courtenay for school. I looked forward to meeting new people and venturing out of the safety of my elementary school friend group. I planned to join the chess club until I saw the group of awkward-looking boys assembled in the science lab. I promptly decided to find some new hobbies for my junior high experience.

I brought the same need to excel to my church activities. Especially on Bible Quiz days. I performed so well that the man who organized the quizzes insisted that I must have had the same game cards at home. How else could I possibly know all the answers, especially to some of the little-known details of the Bible stories? But no, my secret weapon was a collection of books that depicted every Bible story in comic book form. I read them endlessly—in the bath, the car, and late into the night—soaking in all the details of the characters and stories. But I wasn't just consumed with acquiring knowledge; I was growing in my understanding that there was a God who loved me. And it defined me. I was that kid. The one who would share about my faith with other children on the playground. The one who won prizes at church for memorizing large Scripture passages from the Bible. The one who had an insatiable longing to understand as much as I could about Jesus, a man Christians believe was God incarnate—a flesh and blood human who was also God.

Our family's life centred on God, and our activities revolved around the church calendar. Sundays were for going to church, morning and evening. Wednesdays were for youth group. And then there were the potlucks, picnics, baseball games, and work bees. And, of course, in the summer we went to Camp Qwanoes. My brother, sister, and I each attended kids' camp, but we also went to family camp with our parents. No staying in the lodge for us. A caravan of campers would arrive from our church, and we'd set up together in the corner of a large field, claiming our place as the Courtenay crowd. All our family's closest friends were from the church. It was a place of community, learning, and fun. And it felt safe.

I thoroughly enjoyed my childhood years in the church, except for one activity that was imposed on me: Girls' Club. I didn't want to go, but all the other girls my age went, and my mother was one of the leaders. Attendance was non-negotiable. I had a bad attitude right from the beginning, often being a disruptive smart mouth, chatting when I should have been listening. I didn't want to sing the songs or do the crafts. I didn't want to wear the blue jumper with the red sash. And I really didn't want to fill in all the blanks in the club workbook to earn badges, so I just copied from another girl. When one of the leaders gently confronted me on this cheating, I felt no shame. To me, it was just practical. *You're wasting my time here. I've got better things to do.* So I was asked to leave. I was pleased with this result until my mother insisted that I do the mortifying task of apologizing to each of the leaders. They were gracious about it, and I never had to go to Girls' Club again. Perhaps, in hindsight, this was my earliest resistance to gender segregation.

My faith never wavered, even as a teenager. I had a passion for telling others about God. At a young age, I determined that I would become a missionary and go to faraway countries to tell people of his love for them. I had felt the call. When I was a teenager, our family friend Mr. Ness instructed me gently, "Never forget this spiritual nudge you've received from God." I swore to him that I never would.

But I did.

After high school, I took the oft-travelled route of an ambitious girl from a small town. I moved to the big city of Vancouver. I pursued my education in medical imaging and started my career as an X-ray technologist in one of the city's large hospitals. I married a wonderful man named John and inherited a big Italian family and a "happy" last name (Felice means happy in Italian). Eventually, we were blessed with the birth of our son and then, three years later, a daughter.

Like many other young families, when our first child was born, we moved to the suburbs so we could afford to buy a house.

Once we found the community that would be our home for the next twenty-four years, one of our first priorities was to find a church. John and I visited a few different ones but were discouraged by their homogeneity, as we were looking for a community more diverse in age, race, and economic status. But one Sunday we walked into a church that matched our wish list. It had a lovely medley of people, and everyone was so friendly. It was exactly what we were looking for in a place of worship.

Over the next eight years, we became part of the community there, forming friendships with many other families. Between my parenting responsibilities and my job, I didn't have much spare time, so I had yet to volunteer much at the church. So when the lead pastor, Todd, approached me about a task, I was eager to help. The church was looking for a new children's director, someone who would oversee the Sunday School classes for the elementary school-aged children. When Todd extended the invitation to be on the selection committee to find the right candidate, I happily accepted.

This was a process that could take quite a few months, but the children's classes needed oversight immediately, so Pastor Todd approached me with a proposal: Would I oversee the program until they hired their new staff member? The teachers were all in place, and I would be provided with administrative support from one of the church office employees. If I'm honest, I was a little insulted. I had a real career, one which I was enjoying. My supervisor was even giving me extra responsibilities when she went on vacation, suggesting subtly that one day she could see myself in her position. *Is this something I want to do? Do I have time to take on this extra role? I don't want to babysit the children.* But those thoughts, I kept to myself.

My children were eight and five, and I was invested in what they were learning, so I thought this would be a good exercise. I could learn some things over the next few months and perhaps help other parents do the same. There was a team of competent teachers, and my job was to simply provide the resources and equipping they would need. So I said yes.

I had help from Amanda. She was working part-time at the church while she attended school, eventually becoming a teacher and then a faculty associate in the teacher education program at a large university. As we considered which curriculum to use for the children, we naïvely said to each other, "Let's write our own. How hard could that be?" And we did. We didn't mind the effort and time it took to develop fun but meaningful lessons.

After a couple of months, something started to happen that I wasn't expecting. I began to imagine myself in the job permanently. I was enjoying the role, but even deeper than that, I found it a privilege to facilitate an environment that could help children understand there was a God who created and loved them. Working with the teachers and the other parents, it was my goal to model to the children what it meant to be truly spiritually engaged and not just students of religious instruction.

I shared my thoughts with Todd, and he had not expected this turn of events. He said that he had no ulterior motives when he asked me to temporarily supervise the programming; he hadn't even considered me as a potential candidate. My change of heart and seemingly sudden decision meant that I could no longer be part of the search committee, so I stepped down and entered the process on the other side—as a candidate. I certainly wasn't bored of working as an X-ray technologist, but something was compelling me to move in a different direction.

When I eventually was chosen for the position, my X-ray colleagues expressed surprise. Why would I move from my promising career to become the church's children's director? For a lot less money, too. One doctor was quite blunt about it and, with both disbelief and disdain, asked incredulously, "You are leaving us to go teach Sunday School?"

I found it a bit hard to believe myself, but I was excited.

I was ready to start my new job and eager to educate myself, so it was off to the world of children's ministry conferences. It didn't surprise me that most of the attendees at my first conference were women, or even that most of the speakers were men. I did find it odd though, that the keynote speaker used all car metaphors in his presentation. It might not seem very modern for me to say that women don't understand cars like men do, but it's not inaccurate to assert that cars are typically a passion for men.

Or maybe it's just me who knows little about cars. But when the speaker started to compare something to a carburetor to a room filled with 90 per cent women, I started counting. He included twenty car references in his presentation, and I'm sure the few men in the room (and a few women) appreciated it. But most of the analogies he used in his teaching that day were lost on me. To this day, I still don't know what a carburetor does. I did learn one thing that day though—know your audience. A tip I would find helpful for later.

Pastor Todd and the church board were very accepting of many of the new things I wanted to try—from summer soccer camps to Christmas musicals to the first hip-hop dance performed by the kids on a Sunday morning. Compared to my X-ray work, the position allowed a lot of latitude for creativity. I always knew I had a head for science and enjoyed doing work that was based on procedure and accuracy, but for the first time, I realized how much I enjoyed creating projects that required imagination and artistry.

The freedom to be creative wasn't just limited to the fun stuff. My main priority was to encourage the children in their relationship with God. So one of the first changes I implemented was including them in the main service with the adults. It was only for twenty minutes, and then they would head off to their age-appropriate classes. The children were able to observe the adults in this space and participate in ways that were not possible if they were always sequestered away in the children's wing. The adults got to learn that a little disruption is good for the status quo—because the message should be that at church everyone is welcome, even if they make a little noise or can't sit still.

Another change I proposed was the introduction of family communion. Communion or the Lord's Supper or the Eucharist—its many names within the Christian church—is a sacrament practised regularly in the service. Many famous artists have painted beautiful renditions of Jesus and his disciples at the Last Supper while Jesus gives his friends bread and wine and instructs them to keep doing this "in memory of me." This rite is usually done at the end of the service, so the children don't get to participate. To remedy this, every few months at our church, we did communion at the beginning of the service so that families could participate together. I wanted the children to have positive associations of one of the most important sacraments in our church and not the strange and intimidating impressions I had from my childhood.

I was only five, but my memories of my childhood pastor, Tipton Williams, are quite vivid. His name betrays his English background, but it was his stature and sternness along with his black suits that made him bear comparison with Winston Churchill. Once a month, he taught a Sunday School class to all the young children in the church while our parents attended the adult class. He didn't put up with much guff, and Billy, one of the young boys, didn't put up with much sitting still and staying quiet. There was a communion table in front of the stage that had decorative wooden bars on its underside, and Billy was often put there as a consequence for not participating properly. While the pastor would teach us a story, this young boy would stare out through the cracks with his hands wrapped around the bars. I've never been able to take communion since without thinking of Billy in communion jail. I wonder if he still goes to church.

I'm happy to say that family communion is still regularly practised at my church to this day, and so far, no child has ever had to be put under the communion table for bad behaviour.

My new job as children's director gave me the same happiness that I experienced in my childhood church. My memories of growing up in the church are predominantly positive, and many of the friendships I made back then still exist today. It wasn't until I was a teenager that I was first irked by something in our church. And once again, it centred around communion.

Churches are governed by a board, a legal requirement of any charity. In Protestant churches, church leaders are referred to as elders or deacons, differing with each church tradition. In my childhood church, our leaders were called deacons. My father was one of them, and once a month, he and the other elected leaders would serve communion.

The day came when my mother was invited to be a deaconess, and I was so excited for her. I'm not sure why deacon needed to be feminized, though. Actresses are now referred to as actors with the word taking on a gender-inclusive meaning. The term councillor has replaced councilman and councilwoman—one word to describe the job because everyone is doing the same tasks. But perhaps she was called a deaconess to indicate that there was still a distinction between women like my mother and her male counterparts. She visited the sick and lonely just like the male deacons. She participated on committees like all the other deacons. But the inequality of her position struck me one Sunday morning when I was looking for her after the service and I found her downstairs in the kitchen. I stood in the doorway and watched as she laughed and talked with the other women as they washed the communion cups, the little cups that held the wine or, in Baptist circles, the grape juice—God's much holier drink from the vine. Never did I see her at the front of the church serving communion. Men served the cup; women washed it.

I was so confused. It was the 1980s. Shouldn't a female deacon do what a male one does? And yet my mother seemed so happy in the church kitchen, cleaning up on a Sunday morning. Perhaps she was relishing what seemed, to her at the time, a large leap forward for women.

CHAPTER 4
Fitting In

In the church I was now attending, women were leading in ways my mother could never have imagined. And I discovered some similarities and differences between my job as an X-ray technologist and being the children's director at the church—both predominantly female professions. In both fields, it is still typically the men who are in the upper echelons of leadership, but that is slowly changing, with an increase in female doctors and pastors. But one thing remains the same in both work environments: the objectification of women is still there; it just presents itself differently.

When I was working at the hospital, many male patients would not let sickness or broken bones deter them from speaking inappropriately to me. Whether it was a comment like "I like it when you touch me there" or insisting that the lead apron needed to be lowered, teasingly suggesting that their reproductive organs extended to their knees, they attempted to sexualize a simple medical procedure. But I learned (along with all my female colleagues) to continue working, ignoring the comments, and occasionally having a witty reply for them. When you hear the same rude suggestions repeatedly, you develop a stockpile of quick responses.

Working with the male doctors was different, though. When a forty-year-old cardiologist started referring to me as "babe,"

I was confused. I was only twenty-one and couldn't believe he was serious. To me, he was *sooo* old. But as his uninvited flirtations became more overt, I realized I could no longer ignore his advances. Addressing his impropriety would require more diplomacy; he was my superior and I would have to continue working with him. But when I finally found the nerve to address his behaviour, it ceased.

When I started working at the church, I certainly didn't think I would ever experience these types of aggravations, and thankfully I never did—except for the one time a man "babed" me. He was a visiting pastor to our church, about twenty years my senior, and with every subsequent visit, my inside voice would whisper, "Creep," even though he never said anything offensive to me again. I gave him the benefit of the doubt that he was part of a generation who was yet to stop making nuanced sexist comments to women.

My experiences in the church didn't include men's sexual advances, but I am very aware that many other women aren't as fortunate. Instead, the objectification was of the opposite nature. I have an outgoing personality and enjoy making connections with people. I'm happy to talk to a stranger on a plane or work my way through a church foyer, greeting everyone lingering after a Sunday morning service. And I enjoyed engaging in conversation with my male colleagues. I certainly didn't expect the reactions of apathy and fear that I encountered.

The first time I was ignored was at a conference I attended with the church staff. As I stood in the lunch lineup, I realized that the keynote speaker was right behind me. I enjoyed his talk and felt that it was appropriate to ask him a question, considering we were just waiting for our turn at the buffet table. He gave me a brisk and superficial answer and then quickly turned to the woman at his side and said to me, "Have you met my wife?" After he made his introduction, his body language told me our conversation was finished. He was more than a foot taller than me, so it was very easy for him to turn away and avoid eye contact. I didn't want to be rude, so I chatted with his wife for a few moments before turning forward again, wishing the lineup would move a little quicker as the three of us stood there in awkward silence.

A few months later, it happened again. After a wonderful conference presentation, I queued up with people who wanted to chat with the speaker. He took his time with each of the men in front of me, but as I stepped forward to shake his hand and tell him how much I enjoyed his talk, he turned to the woman at his side and asked me, "Have you met my wife?" I turned to say hello to her, and he slipped away. I hadn't even asked my question. Out of politeness, I conversed with her, but it didn't take me long to realize that this senior lady was perhaps in the early stages of dementia.

I was completely professional, but these men's responses were hurtful. Each conversation (if you can call them that) made me feel that as a woman, I was either so dangerous to their well-being that they couldn't talk to me in public, or I was so insignificant that they'd rather talk to no one than to me.

Many male pastors don't wish to be accused of anything inappropriate. They avoid flirting or spending an improper amount of time with one woman, which is to be commended. But then they take it too far. They avoid real conversations with any women other than their wives, which makes it difficult to connect with them. Some will not even drive in a car alone with a female colleague. Unfortunately, their actions of perceived integrity result in their female colleagues feeling at best excluded and, at worst, temptresses worthy of being avoided.

Even within my own church, I was occasionally treated as dangerous. One day, my husband testily said to me, "Why am I getting all these emails from Henry?" I was working on a project with a man from the church, and we communicated regularly via email. Suddenly, he started copying my husband on every message. John received hundreds of work emails each day, and it annoyed him to be spammed with more. When I spoke to the man about it, he explained he wanted to be transparent about his correspondences with me and felt he was respecting my husband by doing this. John's reply was that he trusted his wife, and if the other man needed that kind of accountability, he should copy his own wife on all the communications. I knew Henry didn't mean any harm with his actions, but who taught him to treat women as dangerous? Our conversations regarding work-related matters did not need to be chaperoned.

These stories involve decent men just wanting to have clear boundaries and show respect to their wives. I understand that. But when a woman is not treated like her male colleagues, it's another form of sexism. Whether a man is being inappropriately forward or he's ignoring you altogether simply because of your gender, both are forms of objectification—the power belongs to the man to dictate *how* and *if* a woman should be included.

The experiences of objectification at the church were more hurtful because there was nothing I could do about them. When a man was rude or aggressive to me at the hospital, I could use my words to stop his behaviour, but it was more confusing when men would ignore me altogether. What could I do? Beg to be included? Or just go hang out with the women? These men in both environments did not treat me as Michelle, the person to get to know. I was simply viewed as that woman—someone to be wanted, feared, or ignored.

Despite the discrimination, the following years working at the church were wonderful. And spending more time with the women is exactly what I did. Every Friday morning, I invited women to come to my home. These gatherings included women from my church, neighbouring churches, the community, and even a local halfway house. Our years of sharing about our faith journeys overflowed into the creation of ministries that cared for the homeless, new Canadian families, and women who had just been released from prison. As much as I wanted to be included in working with the men, spending time with this group of women produced enduring friendships and positive social programs in our community.

After I had worked at the church for five years, the board hired a new lead pastor because Todd had become ill and was unable to continue. Pastor Chris was twenty-nine years old, an age that many church members would feel is too young for the role. But he had been our youth pastor, so the congregation had the confidence that he could do the job. So did I.

In our respective roles as children's director and youth pastor, we were able to get many projects accomplished using our differing skill sets and personalities. We had conversations that revealed our shared passion for faith and the work of the church. And when he spoke of his vision for our specific church, I fully bought in. Before he applied for the job, I was quick to recognize his suitability for the role and told him so. One of the female elders also told him that he was the right person for the job. A year later, he arrived at the same conclusion.

At the time of his appointment, I had already started to branch out into helping our church connect with the community. Children's ministry was running well, and I loved dreaming up and starting new initiatives. I knew that my job description was restricting my potential, and Chris did as well because one day he called me into his office.

"It's you I need to work with," he said. "I need to move you into new responsibilities, including a title change."

But not everyone agreed. "She's been hired to work with the children." "There's no more money for extra staff if she moves out of this position." Back and forth, Chris would argue with a few others in leadership. Chris recognized my skill set, and I think the others did too, but "That's just not how things are done. You were hired for one thing and that's the one thing you will do." I was forty-four years old, so the push-back was just an annoying obstacle; it didn't deter me from insisting that I was capable of much more than my job description. I knew my potential, and now Pastor Chris was asserting that he did too. Certainly the others would trust his opinion.

The debate went back and forth between Chris and the others. I spoke my mind boldly with him but didn't get involved in the argument with the other leaders. Until one day, I just stopped. I was in Chris's office as he got off the phone from another difficult call on the subject, and he seemed tired and discouraged. I noticed his resolve start to wane. We talked about the predicament, and in his frustration, he suggested that I just go ahead and start working in these other areas anyway, without a job description or title change. In his exasperation over the problem, he challenged me that a title shouldn't matter. Isn't everything I do for God? I shouldn't be concerned about what anyone called me. I responded gently, neither agreeing nor disagreeing, but the remark bothered me. I didn't need a title for my ego, but why shouldn't it be given to me if I was doing the work?

I realized at that moment that this issue was becoming too much for him. He was brand new to the job. He was half the age of the people he was disputing with. He had many other things to do rather than argue on my behalf, and this was consuming too much of his time and mental energy. He was very competent, but this was a stressor he didn't need as he started his new position leading the church.

So I made a decision, and in September of 2010, I wrote a letter to the church board. In it, I spoke of my love for our church and community and how I didn't want to stop the work I was doing. I explained that my vision and passion had grown beyond the parameters of my job description, so I had a proposal for them. I would stay in the job until they found someone new; after that, I would return to work as an X-ray technologist two days a week, but the other three days, I would volunteer my time at the church continuing to do the work I enjoyed. For me, the most important thing was to do what I loved, even if not compensated for it.

I was at the board meeting when my letter was read, and the elders were genuinely surprised and saddened at my decision, but there wasn't much of a push to problem-solve a way for me to stay. One board member, in his attempt to provide a way for me to still officially be considered staff, suggested I be paid a stipend of one dollar per month. Seriously? If I wasn't permitted to work within my passions and capacity at full salary, I wasn't going to do it for a dollar. But I didn't speak my mind; I just politely declined.

After the meeting, one of the female board members approached me and expressed how proud she was of me to act with such integrity. She had always been a thoughtful and likable woman. But somehow her words of encouragement didn't sit well with me. They seemed to echo the message I kept hearing as a woman. Do your work quietly, don't stir up any trouble, and work for free… rather than fight for what is right.

I didn't want to be told "Good for you." I wanted someone to stand up for my right to be there. But, hey, she'll work for free. And so it happened: I resigned… for the first time.

CHAPTER 5
An Assignment from Dr. Love

When my children were school-aged, I had my "annoying mom" thing I would do every morning when they hopped into the car: "It's time to take these fools to school." My favourite little joke was always met with an eye roll and a groan, but in the fall of 2014, it was time to take this fool to school. Encouraged by my husband and the pastors at my church, I enrolled in seminary to do my master's degree. I was eleven credits short of a bachelor's degree, but my years of experience combined with the fact that I was already leading and preaching in my local church granted me status as a mature student. Accredited establishments can admit a few students each year under this category. It had been three years since I had resigned from the children's director position, and I was ready for something new.

The choice of seminary was obvious. I attended ACTS Seminaries, where the other pastors from my church were working on their graduate degrees. Located in Langley, BC, it was only thirty minutes from my home. Also, I liked that it is a partnership of four different Canadian denominations, because this would allow me to learn outside the bubble of my own faith tradition. (In the Protestant tradition, churches work together under a national leadership. Anglican, Baptist, and Lutheran are examples of different denominations.) A graduate degree isn't necessary to work at a church, but I knew that courses on leadership, the Christian faith, and the Bible would be invaluable for whatever was next for me.

Orientation day was exciting and a little overwhelming. I was in the lineup to get my library card when a classmate confided in me that he was quite nervous because he had been out of school for five years. *Try twenty-five years!* But I held back that comment, and like any forty-seven-year-old mother would do, I assured him that he would be just fine.

I hadn't written a proper academic paper since high school, so I needed to employ the "fake it until you make it" method. I took advantage of a free essay-writing class to refresh myself on the basics. At the end of the course, I asked the teacher in what order we put the bibliography. "Alphabetically, like always," she responded. "Of course." I indicated with my response and body language like I knew it all along but just wanted to check to be sure. But I didn't know. I hadn't written an essay in thirty years.

The school also had free writing clinics for grad students, which I eagerly took advantage of. It's humbling to have a twenty-something-year-old teaching assistant tell you what's wrong with your essays. *What do you mean there's too much emotion in my writing?!* My passion and expressiveness needed to be toned down. I learned that academic writing is less about my thoughts and feelings and more about the facts. For the first year, I had every paper reviewed at the writing clinic, and my writing skills improved dramatically with such helpful oversight.

During my first year, I had another strategy to teach me how to write well. I would select some of the smartest (in my estimation) yet amiable classmates and, after our papers were submitted, would express how much I'd like to read theirs: "What is your topic? How interesting! Would you mind if I read it? I promise not to pass it on to anyone else." Flattery is an effective tool, and soon I had accumulated a collection of well-written essays that I could study for format and style.

Being a newcomer to the world of academia, I approached my first theology essay with nervousness. The assignment was to write about the theological implications of something relevant to my life at that time. I didn't realize—what most of the class already knew—that this meant I could write on any topic. Not knowing this, I tried to honestly assess what was pertinent in my life in that moment, and the most obvious thing I could think of was being a woman in church leadership. Thankfully, I had just finished the mandatory class on how to do research and was equipped to scour the academic books and journals to discover what people smarter than me thought on the subject. We were only allowed to cite authors with doctorates. No one was interested in my opinion. Imagine that!

One of the challenges I encountered was learning to research both sides of an issue. I had to read why intelligent people believed that women shouldn't lead in the church, and then I had to assemble and present all this information and argue for the opposing viewpoint. Ugh! It was all the arguments that I had heard since I was a young girl: God created man before woman. The Bible says women are to submit to men. Gender hierarchy is God's plan.

As much as that process was difficult, I did appreciate how much it encouraged my critical thinking. You can't simply discount other people's opinions before you reflect on them, amalgamate them with others who think the same way, and then write about your findings in a concise, persuasive presentation. It was much easier to defend the side of the argument that I agreed with, and perhaps I got too carried away, as my professor noted that my arguments were well put together even though they were a wee bit one-sided. Yep. I was only beginning to learn to put my biases aside as I researched topics that were important to me, learning that you can't know what you believe until you fully understand alternate viewpoints.

As I completed the conclusion of my paper on patriarchy and equality for women, a funny thought came to me to use as the closing remark. Is humour allowed in academic writing? My gut said no. The young teaching assistant at the writing clinic cautioned against it. But I went for it. I summarized my arguments and then left the reader with a question to ponder. My final sentence, in which I responded to my own question, was "I am not sure. Perhaps I'll go ask my husband." My professor called it cheeky, but his positive comments (and my good grade) revealed that a little laughter is acceptable even when discussing serious topics.

Midway through my seminary sojourn, I took a course that was one of the most interesting and beneficial classes of my degree. It was called Theology of Suffering, and the teacher was Dr. Love. What a great name for a professor; I'd do a doctorate just to get such a moniker.

One of the assignments was to write an essay on suffering. This time, it really did need to be on a subject that was relevant and specific to my own life. Before starting, Dr. Love required everyone in the class to present him with a synopsis of our topic. I had two options: the loss of my father at a young age, or my treatment as a woman in the church. I chose the latter. This might seem like a strange choice to others, but when my father died of a massive heart attack, the pain from such a sudden loss was acute. Intense. It involved uncontrollable crying and overwhelming grief. But as the years tick by, grief and loss are replaced by memories and fleeting moments of regret. He would have loved to have been a grandpa to my children. In contrast, being discriminated against as a woman is consistent low-grade pain, with moments of high-intensity hurt, that you are shamed into not sharing.

This was a big step for me. I had never shared my hurt with anyone before. I thought of the imaginary pile of pebbles that had accumulated over my many years in church leadership—the pile that I tried not to think about often. Those pebbles represented every time I wasn't included or valued. So I took a chance. And my essay abstract expressed that my greatest suffering to date was the marginalization that accompanied being a female leader in the church.

Dr. Love's response to my topic submission wasn't what I expected. His email said, "Come and talk to me." Did he feel this topic wasn't appropriate? Did I need to change my focus?

I approached him with hesitancy and asked him for his feedback. "Remind me what you wanted to write about again." Confused, I reiterated the theme. "Oh yes, I just wanted to tell you that my wife is a pastor, and I know exactly what you're going through. Go for it."

Relieved that I had a sympathetic ear, I began to write. Even though I was assured of confidentiality, I did not name my church or any people in my essay, as I was still under the illusion that to speak of anyone's wrongdoing would be unkind, even unChristian, of me. It was so ingrained in me to not speak publicly of my experiences. Regardless, I was candid, and the project had much cathartic value.

I named the essay "An Unnecessary Loss?" Yes, there was a question mark at the end, because as I considered the losses collected by me as a woman in the church, I was asking the reader to contemplate whether my experience (and that of many other women) was necessary. Was it possible to live in a world where relationships between men and women were equal rather than hierarchal? Does winning for some people mean losing for others? I used the project to process years of pain and the loss of my first resignation.

My Theology of Suffering class also helped me process the betrayal I even felt by God. Why would he create me a woman but give me skills and passions that were deemed only to be used in the sphere of men? Dr. Love's lectures helped me to reframe these unhelpful thoughts. I learned that suffering can be caused by my own foolish choices. But other times, I'm innocent. Sometimes I may discern the Divine nudge to act, but people interfere with those plans. Just because my suffering is being caused by church people doesn't mean they are right. A quote from writer and philosopher Dallas Willard gave me comfort. He said, "The will of God made plain to us is sometimes not fulfilled because of the choices of other people."[2]

I was comforted by this teaching. All those times I questioned whether I really should be leading at my church... and the doubts that arose when respected and accomplished leaders made it clear to me that they didn't think I belonged... attempted to stop me from fulfilling what I was meant to do. When people get in the way of what is true, good, and helpful, others suffer. My only responsibility was to persevere in what I believed I was called to do.

Little did I know that this essay on suffering would just be the warmup to my healing. I had only dabbled in the game of pain. This class was just getting me prepared for all the unnecessary losses I was about to encounter as a woman in church leadership.

Despite my experience in the church, seminary was a thoroughly positive experience, and if any of my professors held male-only leadership views, they didn't reveal them. Mind you, one of my teachers did use the show *Star Trek* as a metaphor for the church. When I jokingly commented that on the show's third season, the captain of the Star Trek Enterprise was a woman, I thought I had brilliantly worked within his metaphor for how the church was shaping. But I received only a forced

....

2   Dallas Willard, *Hearing God: Developing a Conversational Relationship with God* (Downers Grove: IVP Books, 2012), 272.

smile in acknowledgement of my "funny." Hmmm. None of my all-male classmates laughed either.

Finally, after three years of classes, reading thousands of pages from books and journals, and staying up way too late to complete papers, I was finished. I graduated with a very good GPA mostly due to hard work, perseverance, and the humility to realize that I was in a bit over my head, but that there's always help if you seek it. I entered seminary with "impostor syndrome," feeling like I didn't deserve to be there, but I graduated with confidence and realized even a doctorate was possible if I was willing to put in the work.

My graduation from seminary was one of the proudest moments of my life. On the day of the ceremony, we lined up in the aisle and crossed the stage when our names were called. After receiving my diploma, I walked to the centre of the stage and took a seat on the bench between the seminary dean and president. I was already wearing my simple black graduation gown, but as I sat between these two university dignitaries, they placed the red velvet collar—the hood—around my neck, signifying the successful completion of my master's degree.

Photos were taken. I could see my family's faces. My classmates. My professors. I was soaking it all in when I felt the tap on my back by one of the men, indicating that it was time for the next person to take their seat. I just wanted to linger there a little longer and relish the moment. It felt outside of time, a celebration that included no discrimination. I had earned the same degree as all the men, including Pastor Chris, who graduated on the same day. *Let me sit for a while*, I thought. But I dutifully stood up and moved on.

Graduation was finished, but there was one more assignment that I felt still needed some work. One of my first classes at seminary was on leadership, and in it, we took some of the very well-known personality tests, like StrengthsFinder. I had done some of them before, but one of the tests was new to me. It was a virtues evaluation based on Galatians 5:22–23 in the Bible. These verses say that when we live life with God's help, we will manifest love, joy, peace, patience, kindness, goodness, faithfulness, gentleness, and self-control.

Across the board, I tested low in joy.

As I reflected on the six previous years since my resignation from the church, I knew this assessment was true. I loved my schooling, and the volunteer work I was doing through the church was satisfying. But every Sunday as I sat in the pew with my family, I was overcome with melancholy knowing that I was meant to be on staff at the church. It wasn't because I relished being the point person or that I craved public speaking, but it was because I felt with every ounce of my being that I could help lead this group of people well.

Many Sundays, I would come home from church and have an afternoon nap, about two to three hours long. It wasn't until years later that my husband mused, "Do you think that might have been depression?" I think it was.

School was done. Now it was time to go find my joy.

CHAPTER 6
Pastor Michelle

The timing was perfect. Just as I graduated from seminary in 2017, my church's associate pastor, Richard, accepted an invitation to lead a church in Vancouver. His position became available, and I applied for the job. After months of interviews and candidating in front of the whole church, the church members voted me into the position with almost unanimous affirmation, which meant that the fellow in the back row who expressed his silent displeasure during the Q&A session was in the minority. After all these years, were the pieces of the puzzle finally falling into place for me? It seemed so.

Once again, I was employed at my church. The transition into my new position was seamless, as I already knew the people, had developed friendships with the staff, and was familiar with how the church operated. And Pastor Chris, who had only just started in his role when I resigned from the children's director job, was now well-established in his position. My responsibilities were to care for the spiritual and sometimes emotional and physical needs of the congregation, assist with the Sunday services, support the rest of the staff in their areas of influence, and my passion project—get people's butts out of the pews and into the community.

Finally, I had the freedom to work on the projects that were initiated during my time as the children's director with my Friday morning friends—the women who had met at my house every week. One of the women, Michele (the Michele with one "l"), is a humble hero whose entire life is saturated with helping others. When our ladies' group discovered that she was going into the woods by a local park to hand out sandwiches to people sleeping under bridges and in the surrounding forest, the women wanted to help, but a good dose of caution made us hesitant. We suggested that there must be a safer way to do it. To our pleasant surprise, a church close to where many unhoused people congregated happily gave us the keys to their building. While I was still the children's director, we had access to a kitchen and a large eating hall, where we greeted our guests every Sunday evening for three years until we eventually turned the program over to the host church.

We called it SoulFood. One of our key principles was that we weren't there to just serve a meal but to eat it with them. We didn't stare at the guests from the kitchen. We served the food, grabbed our plates, and found a place at the table with them. We knew more than their names; we knew their stories. One week, there was even a marriage proposal. There was no ring but only a man's heartfelt desire to make a life with the woman he loved. They had just both quit doing heroin.

Eventually, this new venture transformed the culture of our church. Yes, there were the naysayers; people from the church told us that we were only providing a "bandage" to the problem. But our goal wasn't to solve poverty; we simply wanted to show love to hurting people in our community. Over seventy people from our congregation formed teams to make and serve meals, visit with our guests, and help them with their practical needs. Our church grew past just viewing poverty as an issue that needed to be addressed and started to embrace that the poor and marginalized could be our friends.

So when our church was invited to join a partnership between the city and a local charity to improve conditions for our new friends, we were quick to support this new initiative. The proposal was that five different churches in the city would care for the unhoused for one month. It was called the Cold Wet Weather Mat Program (the Mat Program), in short, because of the mats we provided for our guests to sleep on. The local charity provided the mats, the nighttime security, the drivers who went to pick up the unhoused, and the overall organization of the program. The churches provided the volunteers who made dinner and breakfast plus a bag lunch to sustain them until we saw them again the next evening. For five months each winter, unhoused people would have three meals a day and a place to sleep.

It was a great plan, but there was also strong opposition to it. The city council meeting when the zoning changes were proposed lasted until three in the morning. The Parent Advisory Council from the elementary school across the street from our church sent a delegation over to express their great concern for their children. And a neighbourhood man stood at the daycare entrance of the church to warn the parents that *these people* would leave needles in the playground and harm their children. The city did approve the plan, and I knew it was a success when a daycare parent inquired when the homeless would be staying in our church and I was able to inform her that that had already happened the previous month. No one had even noticed their time with us. And other than a brief reprieve during the COVID-19 pandemic, the Mat Program still runs today.

I'm still in touch with some of the people I met during those years. They call to share about their grandchildren, their court cases, and how long they've been sober. One man introduced me to another group of people who are typically part of the nameless masses—prisoners. Not only did we see him at the SoulFood dinners, but he also started to attend our church. This was not a simple task, as our church was a distance from the downtown core, where the unhoused congregated.

After not seeing him for a few weeks, we discovered that a parole violation placed him back in prison. When Michele and I went to visit him, he was surprised we came and told us that he never planned on returning to our church because he was so embarrassed that he was back behind bars. Fortunately, our visit reassured him that our friendship wasn't dependent on that. A few months later, when he was released to a halfway house, he was visited by a federal chaplain, who, upon hearing that our friend was a person of faith, asked if he'd like to find a church to attend. Our friend insisted that he already had a church. And that's how we met Chaplain Pascal.

Pascal had an idea to help other prisoners get connected in churches when they were released from prison. He called it High Five Groups. He met with Michele and me and presented an invitation: "I have parolees who want to attend church but can't imagine coming on their own. They feel that when they walk through the front doors, everyone sees the giant F—felon—on their foreheads." Pascal planned to put together groups of five people who would befriend parolees upon their prison release and help them acclimatize their way back into the community, specifically the faith community. Often when individuals are released from prison, their previous friends and relationships are unhealthy for them, so this would provide them with new friends. So Michele and I invited three other women to join us, and we formed our first High Five Group. One by one, our group befriended three different women released from prison. They had done their time and now just wanted to move on with their lives.

Sometimes we would meet the women before their release. Once, Pascal asked our High Five Group if we'd like to participate in the women's prison church service, and he asked me if I would preach. On that Sunday morning, I presented a parable to the women, a fictional story in the Bible that Jesus used to teach a truth. It was about a man who had been forgiven a great financial debt, but when another man didn't pay back a much smaller debt to him, he had him thrown in prison. I posed a hypothetical question, "Why would the man do this?" For me, it was a rhetorical device, so I wasn't expecting one of the women to yell out, "Because he's a jerk!" (Her language may have been a little stronger.) She wasn't wrong. And my heart lit up. What fun to be here with women who were authentic and didn't fear expressing their thoughts out loud.

I gained an understanding of our local prison system during those years. I realized how similar these women were to me, save some bad choices that they were now paying the penalty for. One of the things I learned about many of the women was that they weren't dangerous to the public. So many of them were in prison under the category that I called "dumb things I did for a man." Slipping a little package across an international border because your boyfriend asks you to does not end well. If I felt any judgement for them, it quickly dissipated when I heard their life stories and realized that were it not for the childhood and the fortunate family I was born into, maybe my life would be similar to theirs.

I wasn't so different from them. They had the same desire to belong as I did: to not feel like outsiders, to be loved for who they were. Ironically, it was these marginalized groups of people who always made me feel accepted. I never had to do anything special to be embraced as their friend.

About a year after I started in my associate pastor role, I discovered still another group of people who didn't feel like they belonged within our faith community. They were people who had attended our church for years, but their struggles remained secret. And their pain was great.

One Sunday, I asked an elderly gentleman how he was doing. "Not well," was his reply. Thinking it was arthritis or mobility issues, I asked questions about his physical health. "It's not that. I'm not doing well emotionally." The vulnerability of this dignified older gentleman surprised me. But it was this encounter that spurred me on to seek resources for those struggling with mental health.

The first opportunity was at our annual women's retreat. Every October, the women of our church would go to Cedar Springs Retreat Center, just across the border in Washington State. It was decided that the subject for our time away would be an introduction to the topic of mental health. As we crossed the border, the American guard asked us where we were going. He was very familiar with the nearby retreat centre and inquired about our theme for our weekend.

"Mental Health," I told him. "Oh, that's very good. I have a friend who recently attempted suicide." The border guard had the physique of someone from the military. *Did they serve together? PTSD?* I wondered. For a moment, I thought he was going to open up and start talking with us about it, so I expressed my sympathy. Until his next comment: "Yeah, people need to talk about mental health, especially you women." I heard one of the women in the back seat gasp, but we all bit our tongues because we wanted to get across the border.

Our weekend started with a presentation from a counsellor who spoke about mental health. But after that, it was the women in the church who shared their stories. There was the woman who shared that anxiety descended upon her in her senior years, taking her by surprise because she had not experienced it before. A young mom spoke of being gripped by post-partum depression after the birth of her second child. One woman said her obsessive-compulsive disorder made it difficult for her to leave the house. Another woman shared the shame she felt because she couldn't explain what triggered her panic attacks and suicidal ideation. A daughter shared that she didn't understand her experiences of anxiety until her mother explained how she struggled with her own mental health. I felt so privileged that these wonderful women would share their painful experiences with us—not simply so we could understand what they were going through, but so that we could have some awareness of our own emotional health.

There was also one man who spoke to us. He was the teenage son of one of the women. When he heard about the topic for our weekend, he offered to share his story via pre-recorded video. But only, he told his mother, if he didn't have to sugarcoat it. He wanted everyone to hear the reality of his mental health struggle.

On Saturday evening, after all the talks were presented, we would normally be visiting with our friends, playing board games, and engaging in other evening fun. Instead, the women sat in groups talking about what they had just heard and sharing their own stories. A few brave people inspired the rest of us to share what was going on in our own lives. They gave us the gift of going first.

The weekend had been so impactful for everyone that I started to consider how we could provide this kind of information and sharing with the whole church. How do we include the women who weren't able to come to the retreat? And the men? How do we start the conversation with everyone?

I connected with a local group in Vancouver called Sanctuary, which helps churches navigate the conversation on mental health.[3] They were invited to do a workshop after the Sunday service. I wondered if people would stay for the seminar after already being at the church all morning. I didn't realize the scope of its success until someone commented, "What other topic would convince 75 per cent of the church to stay for another two hours?" The place was packed.

....

3   Sanctuarymentalhealth.org

To follow up, we soon had a Sunday morning dedicated to the topic of mental health. Once again, we interviewed people on video and shared their stories with the congregation. It was the first time the men were hearing from other men. A story of depression. Another man spoke of suicidal ideation. A couple shared their story of support as one partner navigated depression for many years.

And then I got to preach. I shared an insight I received while away on the women's retreat. In the Bible, there's a story told of Jesus observing people as they give money to the temple.[4] The rich people gave large amounts, and it pleased them when others noticed their generosity. But a widow came and gave two copper coins. Jesus turned to his friends and said that she had given more than all the rich people because it was such a sacrifice for her. Perhaps that was the only money she had. God looks at the heart, not the amount given.

So what did this have to do with mental health? I pulled out some correlations: The woman lived with stigma; widows were often poor and considered a burden to society in those times. The woman likely thought she had nothing significant to offer. What could her two coins do for the mission of the temple?

And then I addressed the people in the room: "Some of you were here early and enthusiastically to help with the music, the coffee, or the teaching of the children. Others may have a bit more difficulty getting here, and arriving on time is a big accomplishment. Still for others, it has taken every ounce of mental energy you can muster just to be here. You weren't sure that you would even come. You arrive a little late and leave a few minutes early so you don't have to talk to anyone. You think that you have nothing to offer others and feel burdened by the stigma associated with your mental health struggles. Some people are here

....

4   Mark 12:41–44 (NIV).

with an abundance of good mental health, and that's wonderful. Others feel like all they have to offer are their 'two copper coins.' But God sees the heart; he knows the sacrifice you have made. In this sense, people with mental health struggles often give more than those with good mental health."

A woman approached me after the service. She said it was the first time she felt fully accepted at church. And that brought me joy.

CHAPTER 7
The Butler

When a woman enters a field that has predominantly been occupied by men, she needs to decide how to present herself. The message that I consistently received from both men and women in the church was to never assert myself. Their idea of wise counsel was to advise me to simply do my best in an environment of discrimination and persistent micro-aggressions. Ignore those comments. Be patient. Work hard and wait to be recognized. Don't try to self-promote or ask for what you deserve. When the time is right, people will notice your skills and character, and you will be rewarded. I heard stories from female leaders in other churches who followed this instruction. "I worked years without title or compensation, but then all my hard work paid off and now I'm in the job of my dreams." In hindsight, I now know that this is the reward of the few to the detriment of the many.

Patriarchy has existed in the church since the Christian church's inception. Its stringency has ebbed and flowed throughout church history, but it was in the 1980s that male-only leadership made a resurgence in some North American churches under its new name—*complementarianism*. It sounds reasonable. Men and women work together with skills and giftings that complement each other. Men and women are created equal in worth and dignity in the eyes of God, but (and here's where it gets interesting) they have different roles. Men are created to lead in the home and the church and, depending on how dogmatic one is, even in the workplace. Women are always in a supporting role. It is a partnership designed by God, so how can we question it? Even in 2024, when we should be making big steps forward in equality, the Southern Baptist denomination in the United States is revoking the membership of churches that permit women to be pastors, even if they've been in the role for years. One big step back. Complementarianism is just a fancy word for patriarchy, softened to make it more palatable to those who find themselves in it.

If the God-given natural order of things is that women should always be in submission to men, why does that bring unrest to so many women? The answer from the patriarchal crowd is that she is sinful; she is rebelling from the way God created her. So in addition to feeling the turmoil of not living to her full potential, she's told that she is offending God with her desires.

Complementarianism is even supported by some women. Perhaps some are convinced of the arguments that support it. I was quite incredulous when one of my female classmates at seminary wrote her graduating paper on why women shouldn't lead in the church. But I also believe that some women accept this thinking because it fits well with their personalities. They are content to be in supportive roles because that is their temperament. They would be uncomfortable in leadership roles and therefore are untroubled when men occupy all those positions.

When this topic arises, I refer to the hierarchal order of dogs to explain how it makes me feel. As pack animals, there's always a boss and the others defer. Typically, Fluffy or Spot is quite happy to submit to the alpha dog or the human owner (except for in our home, where our little schnauzer Ruby runs the roost). They are content and feel safe in knowing their place, and if the pack order becomes disrupted, it is stressful for them. But I am not a dog. If I was truly created to be always in submission to men, shouldn't that be a place of contentment for me?

I've not spent too much time dwelling on the unnecessary guilt of not acting the way others think I should, as I think it's more of a transgression to not live up to my full potential. I want my light to shine, to be the best human being I can, without someone sliding the dimmer switch down on me.

Fortunately, more people are increasingly embracing the alternative viewpoint on female leadership—*egalitarianism*. This approach also affirms that men and women are equal in worth and dignity, but there is no difference in the roles and jobs they can do within the church (or the home or anywhere else). If someone is gifted to do something, then their gender is irrelevant.

Christians adhere to the belief that two millennia ago, God himself came to earth in the person of Jesus of Nazareth. This allowed Jesus's contemporaries to be exposed to the character and love of God. He was their brother, their friend, their teacher. Even a quick read of the stories of Jesus in the Bible will leave someone who is not familiar with the Christian faith wondering why the church's view of women is so different than that of Jesus. He lived in a patriarchal society that viewed women as second-class citizens. But he modelled a treatment of women that many had not seen before. He spoke with women in public, which was uncustomary of the men of his time. He invited women to learn from his teaching when others thought they should be in the kitchen preparing dinner. And he welcomed them as his disciples. He was a boundary pusher.

I thought Christians were supposed to follow Jesus's example and not the misogynistic and condescending attitudes of many of the church's leaders and theologians over the past two thousand years. Shouldn't we be treating women like he did?

It is encouraging to realize that many people today are saying yes to that question.

I discovered a movie that provided me with a new paradigm of how women need to work together to change the world's perception of them. For my sister's fortieth birthday, we had a ladies' weekend with the family. One evening, we decided to go to the theatre but needed to find a film that my sister and I would like but would also appeal to my mother and be appropriate for my fourteen-year-old daughter. Lee Daniel's film *The Butler* served this need, and two hours later, my head was swirling with this incredible story that gave me a lot to think about. I must preface my thoughts on this film by saying that I acknowledge that the discrimination I have faced as a Western woman pales in comparison to the tragedies that people of colour have endured in their fight for equal rights. But it is the same principles that I have applied to my own story.

The film is a fictional story set against historical events in twentieth-century United States and focuses on the lives of an African American man named Cecil and his son, Louis. Cecil grows up in the cotton fields of the American South. As a young child, he witnesses his father being shot to death because he dares to challenge the White plantation owner. His father fails to take his own advice, "Don't lose your temper with that [White] man. It's his world; we're only living in it." Cecil is taken into the plantation home and trains to be a house servant, skills that eventually lead him to work in fine hotels and eventually the White House. He does well because he learns to serve and not be noticed, to ensure his presence is never a threat to White people, and to possess the diplomacy to never have an opinion other than neutral deference to the viewpoints of those whom he is serving. He perfects the instruction "the room should feel empty when you're in it."

He provides a good living for his family, although he makes 40 per cent less than the White butlers. Every time he advocates for the Black staff at the White House, he is simply told that if he is unhappy with his wage, he can find employment elsewhere. And so he remains. And he persists.

Cecil's son, Louis, comes of age at the height of the civil rights movement. Rather than attend college near home, he insists on attending a southern university. This is difficult for Cecil to accept, but Louis wants to be part of the equal rights activism of the sixties era. His involvement with the Freedom Riders and the Black Panthers results in beatings, clashes with the KKK, and many stints in jail.

Both men want the same thing, but their approach is very different. Cecil works within the system, pushing for positive change, and Louis takes a more direct approach, believing things will not change without forcing the issue.

The story ends with Cecil securing pay equity and promotional opportunities for the Black staff because of his thirty years of excellent service and persistent quiet insistence for equality. He becomes a hero to the Black community at the White House. His son, Louis, becomes a congressman who continues his work for civil rights. His father declares him a hero and joins him in protest to "Free Mandela." His son assures him they will be out of lock-up soon after they are both arrested. The closing scene shows them thrilled and incredulous as Barak Obama becomes the first Black president. Anything is possible.

So who was right? Father or son? I couldn't get this movie out of my head. For most of the story, there was such conflict between these two men because they believed the strategy of the other was foolish. Both men were incredibly brave and principle driven. But they were different people, guided by their life experiences, education, and natural-born personalities. However, it took both types of action to bring change within the civil rights movement.

What a powerful principle to take from this movie. We are all different, but we are a team. We need the women who employ the quiet strategy. They work hard in all they do, regardless of acknowledgement or compensation. They have personalities that harness any desire to engage in conflict. They possess a diplomacy that showcases their wisdom in difficult situations. Men are not threatened by them, so they can influence others in the day to day.

We also need the fighters—the women who are not afraid to speak up, who disrupt the echo chamber, who insist on equality. They work hard in all they do and insist on acknowledgement and equal compensation. They have personalities that embolden them to stand for what is right. They possess the courage that allows them to navigate misogynistic and abusive environments. Men are influenced by their bold leadership.

So who was I like? The father or the son? I felt the pressure to think that the way of the father was the mature and better way to act. Don't cause trouble. Don't stir things up. You are working at a church. Be nice!

Today, when I see people fighting for justice on the news or social media, I sometimes think that a softer word might be more effective because those in charge might not respond to anger. Then I remember that we are all created differently and are called to work for change each in our own way. And sometimes whispers can't be heard. Often a megaphone is the only way those in power will hear.

CHAPTER 8
Good for Women

Who were my mentors? I was sitting in a conference hall, and the keynote speaker asked us to think of the people who had taken an active part in guiding us in our ministry careers. The men in the surrounding seats quickly started jotting down names. But I felt a little stuck. Sure, there had been a few kind men who had encouraged me. But mentors? I couldn't think of anyone. And I certainly didn't know any female church leaders to whom I could go for advice or guidance.

I had always found my female role models in books. My favourite stories are of women who pushed through barriers to lead in their respective fields. My "book mentors" taught me many things: *Don't focus on being accepted in your field; focus on what you feel called to do. Use opposition to propel you forward. Women often create innovative ways of doing things when they are excluded from traditional environments.*

So I sat quietly and thanked those mentors in my head. But locally, who could I talk to? Where were the other female leaders who could share how they navigate in a world led by men?

Regardless of the lack of female mentors in my life, the next couple of years were good for me and good for women.

The women at my church were happy that they finally had a female pastor. Even though the male pastors were kind and helpful, many found it more comfortable to talk about the issues affecting a woman's life with someone of the same gender.

The city's predominantly all-male pastors' group invited me to their monthly lunches. Pastors and priests from a variety of Christian churches met regularly for networking and encouragement. Sometimes, there would only by one or two women in attendance, but the men made us feel welcome.

I preached a sermon one Sunday and looked down at the front row and saw three teenage girls looking up at me. They weren't doing anything except listening, but I found that moment profound. When I was their age, I never saw a woman at the pulpit, but just my mere presence on stage was normalizing it for them. They weren't going to grow up and say to themselves, "I shouldn't preach because that's not what women should do."

I went to a national denominational meeting in Manitoba, and a young pastor's wife told me that she looked me up online and listened to a sermon because she was so excited to know there was a female teaching pastor.

I began to get speaking invitations at other churches, ones that had only male pastors.

I was invited to be on the denomination's national board, and it was affirmed by our voting members across Canada.

In 2018, our church hosted its first Women in Leadership conference, and it was incredible for women. A team of three organized the event: I and two dear friends, Chris and Christa.

Chris was like Cecil Gaines, the father from *The Butler* movie. Twenty years older than me, Chris was a key leader in our denomination's national women's team and the linchpin of the women's events at our church. For thirty years, she organized our women's retreats and other annual events, and there wasn't a woman in the church who didn't consider her a friend. She was part of the generation before me and, therefore, more patient and understanding of church traditions. She was no wallflower but typically used diplomacy when pushing back against the long-held patriarchy of the institution.

Still, she stood her ground when things were important to her. After returning home from a national women's conference organized by the denomination, she shared a story with me. I still chuckle as I remember both her guilt and glee. The event was hosted by a church in one of Canada's prairie provinces, which tend to be more conservative than the west coast churches. One of Chris's duties at the conference was to host the resource table in the lobby of the church. She's one of the most organized people I know and had put great effort into assembling a reading list for conference participants. But the list was deemed inappropriate because she had included books about equality for women in the church. Therefore, she was told to remove it. Imagine! The male lead pastor telling adult women what they could or could not read. What century are we in again? But Chris didn't let it deter her. She obediently removed the reading lists from her resource table in the foyer... and put them in the women's washroom.

Chris controlled her anger, but she did get frustrated. She had been doing this for many years—teaching, supporting, and loving women—and she was going to continue to do so. And she did, up until her too-soon-death to cancer.

And then there's Christa. She's like the son, Louis, from *The Butler*. For two years, she had been our denomination's national director of women. She and her family had been attending one of our denomination's Alberta churches but had recently moved to a new town. When she was invited to present the Sunday message, she was happy for the opportunity to return and teach at her home church.

My gutsy friend preached a sermon against patriarchy on Father's Day. Christa had no idea that anything was amiss until someone from the church sent her a recording of an announcement given the following Sunday. The pastor and all the members of the board were called up to the stage to show their unanimous support for what was about to be said. A board member told the people that Christa presented a progressive political agenda disguised as a sermon, attempting to further the goal of the egalitarian movement. He then addressed the congregation: "We let our guard down. We apologize. Will you forgive us?" He explained that the church leadership could no longer trust her to speak or have any influence at their church and that they were going to reach out to the national executive office about her sermon. The pastor then proceeded to preach a sermon that disputed everything that she had taught the previous week. The other female leaders and I in the denomination watched to see who would stand up for Christa, but no one did anything significant to help. She eventually got a coerced public apology, but the damage was already done.

No one is a caricature of either a diplomat or an activist. Most of us are a bit of both. Christa had the courage to speak boldly, but she is also a kind teacher and leader. She continues to be an adjunct professor at a Christian seminary and, as of 2024, has been ordained in a different Canadian denomination. Christa is of the same generation as me, and we try to be patient with the social change we hope will happen. We dream that this debate in the church will no longer exist for our daughters' generation.

But... seven months before any of this drama happened, Chris, Christa, and I started to imagine what a conference for women leaders would look like. We had the support of our national executive director, and our provincial district minister even changed the date of one of his events so we could have the November weekend that worked best for us. We decided to invite women from Alberta (the adjacent province where Christa resides) and Vancouver Island as well. Would they come? If they did, we'd billet them with Vancouver women and waive the registration fee.

My job was to get on the phone. I knew many of the female leaders in the Vancouver area churches and extended the invitation directly to them, but for our denomination's churches throughout the rest of the province, I needed to talk to their male lead pastors about whom we should invite. My recruiting pitch was straightforward: "Do you have any women on staff? On your board? If not, who are the women in your church with great leadership potential? Or lead as a volunteer?" Most pastors were able to accept those parameters and enthusiastically offered me a few names of women to invite.

Some never got back to me, even after my third voicemail message. I am the persistent type. My favourite response (yes, that's sarcasm) was the email I received with the subject line: "We are a Bible-believing church." His email enlightened me that there were no female leaders in his church nor any women with leadership potential; he didn't believe in such a thing. I guess he was a no.

Regardless, we had eighty-eight women sign up, including nine from Alberta and six from Vancouver Island. We hadn't anticipated that one of the smaller local airlines would have a fifty-dollar seat sale allowing our prairie friends to come. The registration fee didn't come close to covering our costs, but we received thousands of dollars in donations from members of my church, which covered the costs of catered meals and goody bags full of resources.

Our national and provincial leaders, both male, welcomed the women via video, endorsing our gathering with their involvement. Pastor Chris presented a talk on the theological supports for women in leadership. It was important for a man to give this lecture, because we knew that if a woman did it, it wouldn't possess the same authority. We didn't want the women to return to their churches emboldened with teaching only to be told by their pastors that this information wasn't valid because it was presented by a woman. It needed to be done by a man who was respected by the other pastors.

The rest of the weekend was all about women's voices. Chris thoughtfully created a seating chart so that each woman was at a table with seven others she had never met. Christa spoke of the beautiful alliance of men and women working in partnership. But mostly, it was about women sharing their stories with each other. Most attendees were not in formal or paid positions in their churches but held incredible responsibility. The most common comment we heard was "I didn't know other women were going through this too." You could see the relief mixed with joy on their faces.

Everything ran smoothly. The women were engaged with the content, discussing it with the new friends they were making. Occasionally, I would go to the edge of the room and watch with amazement; I was imagining all the new potential mentoring relationships. These connections and conversations were so necessary for all the women. And I needed it too. Being in church leadership made me an insider, but being a woman made me an outsider. Here, I didn't feel like I was on the edges of the circle of belonging. I was smack dab in the centre. I wasn't just included; I belonged.

Everyone was so happy.

Almost.

One woman had a complaint. She approached Christa at the end of the conference and asked why we hadn't given any airtime for the complementarian view, the one that does not support women in leadership. I couldn't believe it. This woman was intelligent, educated, and had a huge influence at her church. She was invited because she was a leader. I'm sure she has her own story of why she felt strongly about this, but she was alone in her sentiments that weekend.

I inquired incredulously of my two partners in crime, "Why? Why would someone ask that? The whole theme of the conference was women in leadership. Why would we spend time or invite speakers to tell women why they shouldn't be leading? That's a message they have already heard for the past thirty, forty, or fifty years of their lives."

After my initial frustration with this woman's critique, I summoned up my empathy for her. Her protests didn't surprise me because I was brought up in the same tradition. I was also aware that she belonged to a church that didn't believe women should be in leadership positions. If all you've ever been taught is one way to think about things, it must be shocking to hear a room full of people affirming a different viewpoint. Hopefully, the conference gave her much to think about as she continues to discern and analyze the teaching and stories she heard that weekend.

Overall, it was a successful conference, and I hope its impact continues in the attendees' lives today. But my biggest wish is that one day women's leadership conferences won't even be necessary—because they will all be sitting in the same room as the men.

CHAPTER 9

Welcome to the Club

My friend Sheri called and invited me for coffee, saying she needed to talk to me about something important. I didn't see her as often anymore because she and her husband, Craig, were on a team that left our church to start a new one. For two years, they were part of this young church's unofficial leadership and supported it with their time, money, counsel, and plenty of enthusiasm.

As we found a cozy spot in a local coffee shop, I could tell she was agitated about something. She quickly got to the point. Starting a new church is a lot of work, and their lead pastor needed a break from preaching each week. He had asked his team for suggestions on who could present the message on a Sunday morning so that he could have a break. Sheri put my name forward. It seemed an obvious suggestion, as everyone knew me from the "mother" church, where I was now the associate pastor. To her surprise, the lead pastor gently said that bringing me in to help wasn't an option because he didn't believe in women teaching from the pulpit. He had written an academic paper on it. "Would you like to read it?" Sheri recoiled, saying, "No, thank you!"

The "daughter" church was now preparing to depart from the parental nest, which meant it needed its own governance board.

Prior to this moment, Sheri had been unaware that this pastor didn't support women in the highest levels of church leadership. And, for the first time, Sheri realized what might happen as the church morphed into its formal leadership structure. Her leadership skills might no longer be needed—simply because she was a woman.

I sat and listened as she shared her story. Her angst was fresh as she processed her shock and sense of betrayal. I metaphorically opened the doors for her to the club I had been a member of for many years. *Come on in. The only dues are being discriminated against because you are a woman.* I could empathize with her pain of discovering the anti-women sentiment that brews ominously below the surface of so many organizations. Finally, the truth had come out.

This revelation was not a shock to me. I was aware of her lead pastor's views because a few years earlier, before I became a pastor, I had been on our church board when he was selected.

When our church decided to "plant" another church, we hoped that its leader would come from within our congregation, someone whose character and skills we were already acquainted with—an individual who was familiar with our church culture but, of course, would have the autonomy to lead things in his (or her?) own way. A few church members inquired of me, wondering if I would put my name forward, but it didn't interest me.

Discussing the church plant and its potential new pastor was on the agenda for our annual retreat. Every year, the staff and board members go to a rural setting to spend time together and vision plan for the upcoming year. After lunch on the first day, we gathered in a meeting room, our chairs in a large circle, the sun streaming through the windows as it weaved its way through the large trees surrounding our building. There was a sense of serenity. As the group commenced talking about a pastor for our church plant, a sudden turn of energy consumed the room as a few elders were bursting to share some good news.

There was a candidate! A man whom they felt was suitable for the role. He was intelligent, kind, charismatic, and devout. He and his wife had been part of our church for a few years, and I liked them both, so I started to ponder this option. He was a good contender, and I started to have a conversation with myself debating the pros and cons of him in this position. He was young, only in his twenties, but I squelched my apprehensions by acknowledging that the passions and energies of the young accomplish a lot. He was also young in the faith, and to me, this was more of a worry. He hadn't grown up in "church world." Was he prepared for the typical obstacles and doctrinal debates that arise in most churches at some point? Would people who had been in the church for much longer than him be willing to follow his leadership?

I did not even have a moment to ponder these questions or present them to the rest of the group because there was almost instant affirmation from everyone in the room. I was surprised because most of the team was receiving the news at the same time as me. There were a few men who had known of his candidacy for a couple of months because this young man had invited their counsel as he considered the role for himself. But for the rest of us, we were hearing about it for the first time. Even so, the consensus of those in the room seemed to leave no doubt that he was the man for the job.

I wanted to speak up, but he was present among us. This potential new pastor had been one of the elders at our church because we have always been very good at providing leadership opportunities for promising young people. I wasn't opposed to him in this role but was simply overwhelmed in the moment because of the church leadership's immediate approval of him. Everyone in the room was excited, and the candidate was right there. He had given the role much consideration and sought discernment and advice from others. So how could I interrupt everyone's excitement with my questions? Especially when it seemed like I was the only one who wanted to talk about it.

At such joyous news, someone suggested we pray together and thank God that we had the right person to lead this new church. I bowed my head and played the part, but inside, I couldn't pray. I was thinking back to the time when I resigned from being the children's director because no one could envision my role expanding, even though, at the time, I was doing so much more than my job required—even though it was Pastor Chris who requested it. This was a completely different scenario, but the contrast between his situation and mine was unsettling for me. It seemed that everyone in the room could imagine what this man could do—something that they weren't able to do for me.

Also, where was the discussion about this choice with the group? Ironically, our church board had just finished a study on how to make decisions together: slowly, thoughtfully, working as a team. But all that seemed to be irrelevant when this bright, magnetic, and dedicated man stepped up to the plate. *Here you go. We will put you in charge of a whole church.*

The time approached quickly for the launch of the church plant, when a small group of people would leave our church to start this initiative. My husband and I had been asked many times if we might join this new group because a start-up needs both youthful enthusiastic individuals and experienced mature ones. We always said no. And I never honestly told others why we chose to decline.

My refusal to be part of this project was because I was aware of one fact that was undisclosed to most of the people in our church. Our new pastor for the church plant believed only men should be in leadership. Why would I be part of a church where I would never be able to use any of my God-given talents? Why would I want to bring my teenage daughter there? It might be a "secondary" issue for some (not of primary theological importance), but if you're a woman, it infiltrates every part of who you are. I liked this new young leader; I just didn't agree with his thoughts on women in leadership.

I shared my worries with a few people on the board and staff, but they did not resonate with my concerns. I was told that the topic of women in leadership was of little consequence compared to the project of starting a new church. My hopes for women in this new venture were even dismissed by a few women, and I suspect it's because they didn't view themselves as leaders, so it wasn't their fight. As my apprehensions were completely shut down, I felt the guilt of "doing the right thing." Maybe it was time to be more like Cecil Gaines rather than the son, Louis, from *The Butler* movie: stay within the system and work for positive (yet slow) change. So when some of our dearest friends decided to be part of the launch group, I kept my thoughts to myself because they were so excited. It was not my job to sow dissension.

The church began. All was good. For two years, this new congregation was excited about the community they were forming and the work they were doing in the community.

Then Sheri called.

Not long after that, my phone rang again.

A female voice earnestly asked, "Can you come over to my place and teach us about why women should be able to lead in the church?" The "us" was a group of young, educated, and competent women. I knew them because we had all previously attended the same church, and now they were part of the new congregation. Just like Sheri and Craig, these young women, along with their husbands, had partnered with the founding pastor to establish this new venture. And just like Sheri, they had only just discovered that things might change drastically.

In a few weeks, there would be a meeting to determine whether this church would have an all-male board or would it allow females. *Allow!* These women had been part of the de facto leadership since the church's conception, and now they were having to prove they deserved to stay there. They had called me to help them understand Christian theology surrounding the topic so that they could attend the upcoming leadership meeting equipped to state their case.

"Of course, I'll come, but please keep our rendezvous to yourselves." As I spoke the words, my hesitation seemed ludicrous. Why did this meeting have to be in secret? Probably because it had been bred into me not to be a troublemaker, but isn't trouble being made by continuing to believe that capable women need to be "allowed" to do the same as their male counterparts? Why is "men only" the default setting?

I could feel their pain, their angst about being excluded. I had already travelled this road over the previous twenty years and knew what was ahead for them. I was used to the constant prohibitions and limitations women encounter in the church but now was witnessing a new generation navigating similar obstacles.

We met in one of the women's living room. Their toddlers ran around while we sipped tea and talked about theology. I brought scholarly books that would best help them in their preparations. It was a wonderful afternoon of camaraderie, and I tried to subdue the hopelessness I felt for them while encouraging them to fight for what was right.

A few weeks later, I inquired about their meeting, and they were overjoyed to share that no arguments were needed. Their pastor, who had originally been an adherent of the male-only camp, had done his research and changed his mind. Women and men would work together in leadership at this church.

Whew! Things were changing!

And my cynicism melted just a little.

CHAPTER 10
Unexpected Curveball

In the summer of 2018, Pastor Chris took a well-deserved three-month sabbatical. Our denomination encourages churches to offer time off to their leaders because being a minister is an emotionally taxing role. During his absence, I assumed his duties, and it was a good test of my abilities to oversee the running of the church. When he returned, he told me he had been able to truly relax knowing that everything would be fine under my care. It meant a lot that he had such confidence in me.

Our work partnership had been a healthy one. He was an intellect whose passion for study and teaching enabled him to skillfully serve his congregation, but he also cared and connected well with people. He had a lot of ideas, and one of my key strengths was "getting things done," equipping the people in the church to work as a team to bring his ideas to life.

He permitted me a considerable amount of freedom in my leadership and care of the congregation. Never one for routine or maintaining the status quo, I would sometimes surprise both him and others. I liked to try new things during the church service to wake people from their Sunday slumber. But he never gave me grief. Besides, he was always the one to cite the well-known saying that it's better to ask for forgiveness later than for permission in advance.

Finally, I felt like I had arrived at the destination. There had been many changes over the previous ten years. I had earned a graduate degree. My husband and I both changed careers. The children were launched and out on their own. We sold the family home and were building one that was better suited for just two people. And now, my work life had steadied into a nice rhythm. I loved going to work each day and truly cared for the people of my church. It was such an honour to be invited into their lives as they navigated marriage, parenting struggles, health woes, and celebrations. I had just entered my fifties, and this was surely the prime of my career.

While Chris had been away, he had time to rest and reflect on his own life and the direction of the church under his leadership. And it wasn't too long after his return that he surprised me with a proposal. At one of our weekly planning meetings, he told me that he'd been considering the idea of us moving into a co-pastoring arrangement. No longer would I be the associate pastor, but we would be equal partners in the leadership of the church. This arrangement would provide space for him to pursue doctoral work, but also, he said, "This arrangement would help people see you in a different light." It would get them used to seeing me as a lead pastor.

The feelings surrounding our conversation reminded me of when he first invited me to preach, even though I was yet to be a pastor. Scary but exciting. I was nervous but ready to be on this new trajectory. We both knew how difficult it would be for me to get a similar job in another church because most would not even consider a woman for this position. But here was a plan that could baby-step it into action; I could slowly take on more responsibility. And the congregation was likely to embrace the venture because it was Chris's idea. It was an unexpected invitation, but I was thrilled at the prospect of it.

After ten years in the pastorate, I had watched not only his confidence and skills grow but also his belief that a woman can lead in the same capacity that a man can. I knew he trusted me and believed in my abilities. He had always been one of the few who recognized my potential when others couldn't.

Chris hadn't chosen a date for this transition, but every time I thought about this change in our partnership, I was excited by its wonderful implications. I relish challenges and find nothing more motivating than knowing that there are new things ahead. I can survive in the role of manager, but it's not my sweet spot; I love to envision new ideas and bring them into action. Over the next few months, I never inquired about his plan because I didn't feel I had the right. It was his job, and if he wanted to approach the board about this change, it would be done in his timing. And so I waited.

It was mid-December, and the church was in full swing of the Christmas season. Lighted Christmas trees decorated the stage. I was excited about bringing the message for the Christmas Eve services, and the advent candle had been lit as we all anticipated the special holiday ahead. Chris and I gathered in his office as we did every week for our regular meeting. He said there was something he wanted to talk to me about. I had a sense that it might be important. My stomach started to flutter, but I kept a straight face. Was now the time? Was the upcoming year going to bring amazing new opportunities?

He started to share what was on his mind, and within minutes, he quickly and dramatically reframed what I thought my future was going to look like. "In a few months, I'm going to be leaving my position here at the church," he informed me. He was going to move with his family out of the suburbs and right into the heart of Vancouver. He had dreamed for years about starting a church there, and now it was time. Not usually at a loss for words, I wasn't quite sure what to say and was uncertain what my body language was projecting at that moment. I understood his excitement. A new city, a new project, a new home. It was a brave undertaking. I could appreciate his enthusiasm because we were similar in our eagerness to take on new challenges. Congratulations were surely in order. If I managed to express any good wishes to him, I'm uncertain at how well they were conveyed, as they were overshadowed by my emotions of anger and confusion.

What happened to the plan from a few months ago? Even though his life decisions don't require my approval, how come this is the first time I am hearing about this? What would this mean for the church? What would it mean for me? I was processing so much in my mind all at once that it was hard to restrain my emotion, and after ten years of working together, it really wasn't necessary. We had always been honest with each other. I told him of my ambivalent feelings surrounding his news and my disappointment that he had not shared it with me earlier. He nodded. He had wanted to tell me sooner but hadn't, because he knew out of everyone (staff, board, congregation), his plans would impact me the most.

He decided to wait to tell the congregation until after Christmas, so "What's next?" was put on hold for a few more weeks. My feelings needed to be compartmentalized as we proceeded with all the holiday celebrations. When the church family was eventually informed, they were both surprised and saddened about his upcoming departure. But Chris quickly rallied them into supporting his new venture and all the good things it could bring to the city.

We had a wonderful farewell celebration for Pastor Chris and his family, allowing everyone a chance to say goodbye and wish them well on their exciting new endeavour. There was cake, a commemorative video, and funny gift presentations from the staff. His favourite TV show was *The Office*, so we each shared some of our "Michael moments" about him, mostly about treats being pilfered from our offices to satisfy our boss when he needed a snack.

With his departure, the board now had a lot to manage, with the foremost challenge being to find an interim pastor. The search process for a new lead pastor can take about a year, so it was necessary to find someone to guide the church during this transitional time.

For me, it was now time to change my mindset. I had been quite content in my role as associate pastor but knew I could handle more. Unlike when I first started at seminary, I never struggled with confidence with my work at the church. When I was the children's director, I knew my abilities exceeded the boundaries of the job description, but unfortunately, I had to learn that it would take longer for others to appreciate my capabilities. Now that I had demonstrated my competency in my associate pastor role, I was once again ready to embrace increased responsibility. I was already leading the staff meetings, liaising with most of the committees of the church, and was comfortable in the varying tasks of the pastoral role. I too had a vision for this church and felt confident in my ability to love, serve, and lead my church well.

Because of circumstances beyond my control, there would be no baby-stepping; it was time to jump into the deep end of the pool.

I started to imagine the possibilities.

CHAPTER 11
The Invisible Woman

My sister learned at an early age that tears can be effective. During our elementary school years, our little rural school always participated in the celebration of Victoria Day, the long weekend in May, which is the unofficial start to our Canadian summers. One year, my sister was a princess for a day, and she rode the float with the entire royal party. She wore a teal satin dress, a cape trimmed with white fake fur, and a tiara on her head, and she waved her little white-gloved hand as she rode in the parade that day. Every year, a queen and two princesses were chosen for the honour. What I was unaware of at the time was that when my ten-year-old sister discovered it wasn't to be her, she burst into tears. So the teachers decided for that year, instead of two princesses, there would be three.

The tears of a young girl who just wanted to be a princess were effective and make for an amusing story that I still tease my sister about. But as a grown woman working in a man's world, I knew that tears would never help me achieve anything. I considered them to be a shameful expression of weakness. But I had learned a trick to control them.

When I was a newly graduated X-ray technologist, I was looking forward to finally having some money. For three years during my training, I existed on pasta and tater tots and shared clothing with my trendy neighbour so that I could occasionally have something new to wear. Now, I hoped to finally be able to afford to live in the big city, but there was not a lot of work available. Most new graduates had to pick up casual shifts in two or three different hospitals. To try and negotiate some more work, I arranged to meet with the boss of my training hospital and implored him to give me more shifts, as I could hardly pay my rent.

As I spoke to him in his office, my eyes brimmed with tears, but I resisted the urge to wipe them away, hoping he wouldn't notice. He gently explained that he was trying to give me as much work as possible. I feared that my tears would make me seem childlike when I was now a working professional; I was twenty-two and should be taking care of myself. Fortunately, it was not long afterwards that my workload increased and I could rely on regular paycheques.

After that stressful encounter, I shared with a friend how I let my emotions get the better of me in that situation, and she gave me some advice. To stop myself from crying, I should dig my fingernails into the back of my hand. The pain would make my brain focus on what's hurting physically instead of what's hurting emotionally. Turn my hands face up on my lap, and no one will even notice I am doing it. Tears are not something I am easily susceptible to, but over the years, this has been a tool that I have occasionally used during difficult situations. (Never did I view this as self-harm but simply a way to temporarily shock me into not crying.)

Soon after Pastor Chris announced he would be leaving, I discovered that I would need to employ this little aid once again. It was at the first board meeting after the news was shared with the congregation. The elders and I met in the lovely home of one of the board members. The atmosphere was friendly and comfortable as everyone sat with their coffee and snacks, preparing for the evening ahead. The priority agenda item that evening was a discussion about who was going to lead the church during this transitional time. In my heart, I knew it was time for my next step, but thought, *Wait to be invited. Others will acknowledge your work and invite you.*

I had been a member of the church for twenty-three years and in leadership for fifteen. I'd been the children's director, a board member, and the associate pastor. I created key programs and liaised with the leaders of all the different ministries. I was the key connection person with many of our projects in the community. I had been a member of the provincial board of the denomination and was presently on the national board, flying to Edmonton a few times a year for meetings. I represented our church and voted on its behalf at annual national meetings. I had good relationships with each of the board members and staff and had not had any significant conflict with anyone in the church congregation.

The meeting opened, and the conversation began. "I've heard good things about this guy." "This fellow has been a transitional pastor at other churches." "Dr. So-and-So has given us these men's names to consider." I was in shock. I didn't know what to do. Was I invisible? It's not like I expected them to turn to me and unanimously say, "It's you, Michelle, it's you" (well, maybe I was expecting it just a little bit), but why was no one even putting my name forward to be considered with these other unknown men's names?

I was not too young; I was fifty-two years old.

I was not inexperienced; I had proven myself over many years.

No one could say I wasn't a culture fit. I'd been part of this congregation for twenty-three years and participated in creating that culture.

Wouldn't it make sense for me to be the interim pastor? This would be the least disruptive to the church. Isn't it better than bringing in someone no one knows? Why was I not even being considered as one option among all these strangers?

As the discussion revolving around a potential interim pastor was happening, I was enveloped by a familiar hopelessness. My thoughts returned to when I was the children's director when few recognized my ability to do much more than my job description. Memories flooded my mind of how I felt when the young male pastor was so enthusiastically selected to lead our church plant. *Am I delusional? Do I think way more of myself than I should? How is it that I am sitting here right in front of them but apparently invisible?* But I'm old enough and bold enough to speak up for myself. I don't think I could have forgiven myself if I hadn't. So with as much humility and diplomacy as I could muster at that moment, I offered a suggestion: "What about me?"

Silence descended upon the room until one woman spoke up. I can't remember what she said, but she indicated that the board should consider me as well. And then the conversation continued. They were all politely talking about that possibility, but at least I was now part of the conversation. Still, I was somewhat confused. Why was it up to me to suggest that I could be a candidate for the position? It didn't occur to any of the nine other people in the room? I'm someone who likes people to be direct and truthful; I don't need delicate diplomacy. If I'm not suitable for the role, please, just give me an honest explanation.

And then, if the evening wasn't yet uncomfortable enough, my body was having a bit of a "women's problem." I'd had interstitial cystitis for thirty years, an ailment that I'd learned to live with and only occasionally caused me real difficulty. To put it simply, the lining of my bladder gets agitated and becomes so painful that urination is necessary even if there is very little fluid in it. So while I was attempting to act composed, I had to get up and go to the restroom a few times. It would only take me thirty seconds to find relief, and then I would attempt to slip back into the conversation circle without any fanfare.

This added to the stress of the evening. My perception was that people thought I was leaving because I was upset. But it was truly just to relieve my bladder. I wanted to sit in the room, composed, stiff-lipped, professional, being a productive contributor to the discussion. On my third return from the restroom, my humiliation became complete. Some were already on their feet, and one said, "We'd like to pray for you." They must have been talking about me and concluded that I was upset. I didn't want their attention in this way and didn't need prayers for my emotions, but they quickly gathered around me and started to pray. Ugh! I had to fight back the tears; my fingernails deeply embedded in the back of my hand… because I was so angry! They were trying to be kind, but all I felt was their condescension. I was angry at myself for allowing a few tears to well up in my eyes as they prayed for me. I was angry that my bladder betrayed me. The whole scenario made me feel completely pathetic. I felt like they were saying, *There, there, we care for you.* In the moment I most needed to present myself as a leader, they only saw me as a weak woman.

There has not been a worse moment for me at that church before or since that evening. I went home and cried, the only time I have shed real tears over being a woman in leadership. I was used to being treated "less than" for years. I had weathered people's overt and discrete discriminations. With each insult and condescension, I imagined throwing another pebble onto the pile. I could handle it. When I was out with my girlfriends, we'd laugh over the crazy things people would say and groan collectively in recognition of men's patronizing ways toward us. The laughter was a balm releasing the hurts and allowing me to breathe because I was with others who understood and empathized with what I was going through. The "pile" doesn't go away, but it is tolerable when friends carry the weight of it with you, even if it's only for a moment.

My tears that night were about the complete hopelessness of my situation. What more did I need to do to be seen? I also carried the humiliation of being tearful rather than tough when the situation demanded it. I called in sick the next day. A lot was about to happen in the next year, and in hindsight, I feel no shame about how I conducted myself in all those situations except for that one night. Somehow, I wish I had been able to control those tears.

CHAPTER 12
The Owners

I don't know what happened after I left the meeting that night, only that soon after I was given the invitation to be the interim lead pastor. The humiliation of that evening stayed with me as I wondered if the board perceived me as a tearful toddler demanding what I wanted. I took consolation in reminding myself that no man with my experience and the excellent relationships I had with the people of the church would have had to endure what I did. His name would have been part of the conversation right from the beginning, perhaps being the only name discussed. So I chose to push the embarrassment behind me and get to work.

I had one question for the board: "Am I just managing the church during this time, or am I allowed to lead?"

"Lead, please lead," they assured me. I knew the process of selecting a new lead pastor would take at least a year and was excited to see what I could accomplish in that time.

The history of our church and its relationship with women in leadership had been on a positive trajectory since the early 2000s. Pastor Todd, the minister who led our church before Pastor Chris, initiated the first important change. In our denomination, each church is self-governing. A national executive director and a centralized staff give oversight to churches across the country that are united by a shared mission. To be part of the denomination, each church adheres to certain core beliefs, but secondary doctrines—things not of primary importance, such as the question, "Can a woman lead in the church?"—are left up to the individual churches. Every church has a constitution and bylaws that can only be changed by a vote of the membership.

Pastor Todd believed that women should be serving in leadership, and he proposed allowing women to be elders in the church. The other suggested constitutional change was that women could also be pastors in every role *except* for lead pastor. Years later, I asked Todd why he didn't dispose of this one prohibition, and he said that it would have been too much change all at once. He had to start with small steps. He knew that if he included women in the lead pastor role description, the other proposed changes would not get the affirmative vote they needed. That made sense to me, and I admired him for being so ahead of the curve in his respect for women and their abilities.

Still, this newly established equality had its challenges when put into practice. The very first woman invited to be on the board shared her story with me, bemoaning the condition that came with the invitation. Her husband had also been asked to be a board member, and the expectation was that they would participate as a team. It was made clear to her that acceptance onto the board was contingent on her husband also becoming a board member. If her husband declined the opportunity, then her invitation would be rescinded. Of course, her husband was not subject to the same condition. I'm sure, at the time, this was considered a wise way to move forward, and fortunately, it wasn't too long afterwards that women were invited onto the board based solely on their own merits.

Quite a few years later, in 2012, I was attending a board meeting as an elder (not yet a pastor, as I hadn't been to seminary yet), and I chose to address this topic. So many of the pivotal stories in my church career happened in board meetings because this is where the decisions are made, where the power lies in either upholding the status quo or creating change.

Unfortunately (or fortunately, depending on how you view it), I am more bothered with myself when I don't speak up about something than if I do. Doing nothing feels like a negative choice.

Our board was putting the final proposal together for a bylaw change. We were adjusting it to meet new requirements by the government regarding charities. Really exciting stuff. Nevertheless, proper process was necessary, so we were working as a team to make the necessary changes before presenting it to the church members, who would ratify it with a vote.

The bylaws document is not an item that gets read often, and its formal legal format doesn't provide very exciting reading. Still, we needed to review it carefully and make changes thoughtfully because they would then be permanent and binding.

As I started to study the document, I couldn't help noticing a glaring discrepancy in it. The pronouns were inconsistent. Every statement regarding elders used "he" and "she" pronouns. The same pattern was repeated when discussing associate pastors, but as I read the parameters for the lead pastor, only one pronoun was used: He. He. He. I had yet to speak to Pastor Todd, who had initiated these changes many years earlier, so I was confused.

The role of elder is the highest authority in the church, and the lead pastor is considered to be an elder as well, but an ex-officio member of the board. He can participate fully and is greatly influential in the meetings but does not have voting privileges. The rest of the board has greater jurisdiction than him, and if they wish to fire the lead pastor, it's within their power to do so.

As one steeped and studied in Christian theology, I knew the arguments on both sides of the female leadership debate. If our church leadership was agreeing with the reasoning that permitted women to be elders but not employing that same logic for the position of lead pastor, then we were being inconsistent. You can't have it both ways and maintain integrity. This puts forth an obvious question: Why is it acceptable for a woman to be an elder but not permitted to be a lead pastor?

It had been a long evening, and we were almost finished addressing the issues on the agenda. I was feeling bothered, as I wondered why no one else noticed or was concerned by the pronoun discrepancy in the document. Had it become so normative that only men can lead in this position that this inconsistency wasn't noticed, or did they simply not care? I was itching to say something but also knew that it would not be regarded favourably if I introduced a new topic so late in the evening, especially when it wasn't on the agenda. This was not going to be an issue solved in one evening, a simple addendum that would be quickly resolved. The meeting was ending. It was now or who knows when: *How many years will it be until we pull out the constitution again? I must say something.*

OK, not too aggressively now. Be demure. Speak humbly. I recall my exact words: "I appreciate that this is not on the agenda, but I would like to bring one thing up so that it's recorded in the minutes. There is a discrepancy in our bylaws. The lead pastor can only be a man, yet the theology we support to allow a woman to be an elder should also apply to the lead pastor role. But ours doesn't."

No reaction from the room.

"I'm not asking that we do anything about it right now, but I'd like it recorded in the minutes that I have brought this to your attention and disagree with the stance our bylaws present. I don't want a future board years from now looking through our minutes and wondering why this was never discussed."

Nothing. Crickets. An awkward silence that went on too long. A group of mostly male faces looking at me with uncomfortableness, seemingly not knowing what to say. Then, finally, one man spoke up. "Yes, let's record that in the minutes." Another man "seconds" it. Nothing else was said. We moved on.

Was anything accomplished? No, not even a baby step. I didn't feel heard. My comment was acknowledged and put in the minutes, likely never to be read again. I brought this up at a time when it wasn't even relevant to me. I certainly wasn't fighting for this because I thought that one day in the future it would apply to me. This is not how things should be done. When's the best time to prepare for a crisis? Certainly not when you're in the middle of it. Discrepancies in our governing statements needed to be cleaned up.

One evening not long after that board meeting, my daughter came home from youth group and, in disbelief, asked me, "Is it true that a woman can't be a lead pastor in our church?" Another teenage girl had attended the congregational meeting with her parents and noticed this pronoun discrepancy as she perused the printed bylaws for the first time. She inquired of her parents, who matter-of-factly confirmed her observation. This young gal went and shared this news with the entire youth group. My daughter told me that everyone was horrified, both the girls and the boys. I took solace in knowing that the next generation would have little patience for this type of debate.

I could never have envisioned while sitting at that board meeting that seven years later, in 2019, I would be the interim lead pastor at my church. The board was putting a search committee together for a permanent lead pastor, and I intended to apply for the job. Even though many people in the church assumed that I might just move into the role, I understood that I had to go through the same protocol as every other applicant. Just like the other candidates, I needed to be vetted and interviewed to be seriously considered. Even though I knew that it was an intensive process, I felt calm. I was already doing the job. Doing well in the role. And there had been no opposition to me leading as the interim pastor.

In my new role, one of my responsibilities was to attend the annual denominational conference for the province, so my husband and I headed over to Vancouver Island, where it was being hosted. We never expected that one of the presentations would give us a vocabulary that we would start to use in the upcoming months.

The lead pastor from the host church shared some stories of when he was a young minister at his first church. Alone in his church office, he was preparing to give his very first sermon on a Sunday morning when the church accountant came in with his first paycheque. As he presented it to this newly minted pastor, he told him, "I know that you and the board have agreed to a certain salary, but I think it's too much, so I've made some adjustments." The young pastor was shocked and promptly put him in his place, telling him to pay him what was agreed upon. My husband and I, along with the room full of people listening to this story, found ourselves in a position of mixed horror and amusement. Who would do that?

The host pastor continued with his stories. A few people accused his wife of stealing toilet paper from the church for their parish house next door. The truth was that she was simply putting her order together with the church stock order because it was cheaper that way. The issue became so contentious, it needed to be addressed at their annual general meeting. The whole room was laughing and groaning at these unbelievable stories, only funny because they happened so long ago and the pastor who endured them was doing fine now.

The people who were causing him so much grief weren't the staff of the church. Or the elders. Or any of the other elected leaders. But he had a name for them: The Owners. Our host explained. The Owners are often the people who have been around the longest, give generous donations, and are committed program leaders, and this gives them a sense of entitlement that this is their church.

John and I had never heard this term before, but it wouldn't be too long before we discovered that *there were The Owners at our church too*.

CHAPTER 13
A Simple Announcement?

The transition seemed quite straightforward at first. No one seemed to have a problem with me leading the church. The services and programs continued smoothly. Attendance did not wane. Pastor Chris had prepared the board for the reality that many people tend to leave a church when a lead pastor departs. Some follow him to the next church because they enjoy his teaching. Others start attending elsewhere because they don't wish to remain at a church during the upheaval of a transition. To my pleasant surprise, the expected exodus didn't happen. Our numbers stayed steady, which was a great relief to me. Most male pastors who step into a new church expect a decline in numbers and wouldn't be disheartened by it, as it's part of the process during a leadership change. But I thought it spoke volumes that our church's numbers didn't decline under the leadership of a woman. In fact, everything seemed fine until the day of the announcement.

The board had prepared a statement to be read on a Sunday morning. The chairperson found his place centre stage and read his carefully prepared words. He informed everyone that the board had compiled the job description for the lead pastor role and had assembled a search committee. Also, the job was open to any applicant regardless of age, gender, or marital status. His voice conveyed an easiness that indicated that everything was proceeding in the most routine of ways. I'm sure none of the church board had anticipated any fallout from the straightforward communication they had prepared.

The inclusiveness of his one sentence caught my ear. I assumed that the board was making the gentle assertion that the job was open to anyone because they were aware of the pronoun problem in the church's constitution. Behind the scenes, they had decided to proceed with the search process, and if a female was selected as a serious candidate, then they would deal with that discriminatory bylaw. Most of the people in the pews received the announcement without any concern. They didn't even realize there was anything controversial about the statement. Nobody thought too much about it—except for a handful of people.

There are people in the church who are not even aware we have bylaws. There are others who know such a document exists but can't tell you what is in it. And, finally, some people know it well and might even have a copy at home. That's not a bad thing. We should all care so deeply about the church's governance. "The church constitution is very clear. Only a man can be the lead pastor," they asserted. And you know what? They were right. That's what it said.

I was so frustrated. I had brought up this discrepancy in our bylaws many times in the previous years, but my protests were received with a polite acknowledgement and then disregarded. Perhaps because up to that point, a female lead pastor was simply a hypothetical. Pastor Chris was only in his late thirties, and before his resignation, everyone assumed he would be with us for many more years. I imagine there was a sense of "Why create problems when everything is running smoothly? If we just randomly try to correct this bylaw to cohere to ways of practice, that's only going to create unnecessary conflict. Why create problems if we don't need to?"

But I don't see why making things equal for women is an issue to ignore. Avoiding conflict doesn't avoid anything; it just pushes it into the future. All good things take a little pain. But why go to all that trouble for something that's not likely to happen? Except now it was. The time to have dealt with this was before the day I was on staff, before anyone, including myself, could have imagined the prospect of a female lead pastor.

So they spoke up. The people who saw the pronoun discrepancy insisted that women could not even apply for the job because the constitution said a woman could not hold that role. Their assertions were difficult for me to reconcile with the good relationships I had with these church members. Everyone was happy for me to lead the church when Chris went away on his sabbatical. No one pushed back when I was named interim lead pastor, a role that could last more than a year. But permanently? Absolutely not! That was unacceptable.

The board members regrouped and halted the process. It was now time to do something that should have been done a long time ago. The church was going to talk about it. A month later, another elder read a well-crafted letter to the congregation. The board proposed that we change the bylaw that said the lead pastor must be male. He was clear that this was not about endorsing any specific female candidate or even suggesting that the candidate should be female. This was about making our bylaws consistent with church practices and giving the search committee freedom in their search. We'd take a few months, bring in some guest speakers to teach about women in church leadership, have a vote, change the bylaw, and start again with the process. Simple, right?

For many in the church, they didn't understand what all the fuss was about. We'd had female elders and pastors on staff for years. In fact, some people joined our church for that exact reason and likely wouldn't stay if the bylaw change didn't get passed.

There was also another consequence to the bylaw not being changed, but only a few people realized it and spoke about it in horrified whispers. If the bylaw remained the same, it might mean that all our female elders would have to resign. If the theology we adhered to could not support a female lead pastor, then it couldn't support a female elder because both positions are equal in authority, that of the highest level in the church. Moreover, an elder possesses greater authority than a lead pastor because the board has the power to fire him or her. By diving into this topic, we could no longer look the other way regarding which rules we adhered to and which we simply ignored.

I found myself in an awkward position. If this was happening to any of my staff, I would have attempted to protect my employee while working with the church members who possessed varying opinions on the issue. Instead, I had to refrain from taking action and let others take charge. There was a problem needing to be solved, but I couldn't get too involved because I was part of the problem.

The board needed to work through this with the congregation. On a positive note, I considered each elder to be a friend. I was closer to some than others, but I trusted that each one cared for me and would work to resolve this matter. But where did each individual stand on the issue? I couldn't be completely sure. As a woman in the church, unless someone overtly states their opinion, I never truly knew an individual's thoughts regarding women and equality. As elders, they had to support women in church leadership because that's an interview question in the selection process. But for some, was it possible that this issue was not important enough to them to debate? They love their church and will work within the parameters of a church culture that provides equal opportunities for women.

But would they fight for it to remain? Did they care enough to work for justice on behalf of women? Or was there a small part in them that wasn't even so sure what they believed, and if the church voted to remain with male-only leadership, they could work within those boundaries as well?

The protest against the proposed bylaw change started gently. Some people wrote letters to the board explaining their objections to women in leadership at this level. When that didn't get the action they were seeking, they started petitioning the provincial and national leaders. At this point, I don't think my name came up; it was more about the general concept that a women shouldn't be a lead pastor. I knew that there was some general discontent with a few people, but their grievance was with a concept, not with me. I had endured this type of "you don't belong" sentiment for years; it still hurt, but it's the price to pay if you want to be a female leader in the church. Besides, I was too busy in my new role to expend too much energy worrying about something I couldn't control.

As the campaign against changing the bylaw started to become more contentious, my husband made an interesting observation: "It's The Owners." At that moment, we realized that our church had a group of people who were not part of the elected leadership but clasped on to an entitlement that dictated that their beliefs and desires were more important than the majority's. And they were making their voices heard.

I understood the thought processes behind The Owners' objections. They had been taught since they were young that only men should lead in the highest positions in the church. *It says so in the Bible. The Bible says this. We believe the Bible.* But what they viewed as truth, others see as Bible verses plucked out of the text (and out of context) to support certain discriminations.

For example, in the past, the Bible has been used to justify slavery: "Slaves, obey your earthly masters with respect and fear."[5] And "Masters, provide your slaves with what is right and fair."[6] These are two of the verses quoted to remind the oppressed and the oppressor that this inequality was God's idea, rather than the authors addressing the social norms from two thousand years ago. Fortunately, we have moved past the idea that any person should be a slave to another. All humans are equal. It's all about context. Those verses in the Bible were written by authors many years ago for people of another time.

Today, slavery in Canada is illegal, but racism still exists.

Similar to the Bible's supposed support of slavery, it has also been interpreted to speak to a woman's role in the church: "I do not permit a woman to teach or exercise authority over a man; she must be quiet."[7] And "Women should remain silent in the churches. They are not allowed to speak, but must be in submission, as the law says. If they want to inquire of something, they should ask their own husbands at home; for it is disgraceful for a woman to speak in the church."[8]

These verses were written at a time when women had very few rights. They were the property of their fathers and then, eventually, their husbands. Most were uneducated (so learn from your husbands at home and stop interrupting the service). The verses also may have been reflecting some push-back on female-driven goddess cults of that time, which contended that women should be in authority over men. Or the authors simply were influenced by the patriarchy of their day. These instructions are found in letters that were addressed to specific churches in the Middle East. Their intended recipients were never meant to be the Canadian church a couple millennia later.

....

5   Ephesians 6:5 (NIV).
6   Colossians 4:1a (NIV).
7   1 Timothy 2:12 (NIV).
8   1 Corinthians 14:34–35 (NIV).

Today, discrimination against women in the workplace in Canada is illegal, but women are still openly discriminated against in the church.

The male-only leadership adherents will cry for religious freedom: *This is what our God wants.* Although that may have been the uniting thinking of previous centuries, many Christians today are increasingly growing in their understanding of how the Bible works. It's not a magic book that fell from the sky with everything we need to know about God and how to live every single aspect of our lives. It's a collection of stories, poems, and wisdom literature written by people throughout the ages reflecting on their lives with the Divine.

But for many religious people, life is much simpler when God is figured out. Why we think that's possible, I'm not sure. Our study of God comes together with the community we are in, morphs throughout history, and is influenced by our cultural and geographical contexts. I can't remember where I read this expression, but I've never forgotten it: "Bad theology dies one person at a time." It is rare for people to change their minds. A few will, but not the masses.

That is why real change often happens with each new generation.

Now there is a fast-growing movement to understand these verses in their context and appreciate their relevance in our modern world. Women are no longer considered property or inferior beings. They are equal to men, and wouldn't the world be a better place if we all worked as a team? Why would you want to work to accomplish anything and not use every asset you have at your disposal, especially if it means half of your people?

I understand that The Owners believed it was wrong for a woman to lead in the church and they were trying to protect the organization. It wasn't so much that they were against me; it was that they were *for* God. And this might mean that I might get sacrificed along the way. They believed they were "standing up for Jesus," but the problem was they eventually ended up acting in ways that Jesus would never have.

Friends started to become foes. The people who hugged me each week (in the pre-COVID era), thanked me for the meaningful sermons, and shared stories with me in tears as they lamented what was happening in their families were now trying to disqualify me.

The board was on board for a bylaw change.

The denomination supported it.

The Owners did not.

CHAPTER 14
Pebbles in a Pile

Some stories are simply funny. They don't ruin your day or your self-esteem, but they provide you with a good laugh, as they remind you once again that you don't quite fit in. Another pebble goes onto the pile. Another rock that says you don't belong. A rock that doesn't fly up and shatter the glass ceiling but is thrown down and added to the pile. Other stories feel more serious. The intent to slander or hurt you is intentional, and instead of laughter, these hurtful actions risk damaging your self-worth. These rocks bruise. And some even wound.

After the board's announcement about wanting to change the bylaw to allow women to apply for the lead pastor role, the atmosphere in the church started to change. From childhood, I had always felt the safe embrace of being part of a church community, but for the first time, I began to experience the loosening of those arms that brought such security and well-being.

There was a lovely elderly woman who would approach me every Sunday, gently grab my elbow, and whisper in my ear so that no one else could hear, "Thank you so much for what you're doing for women." Now in her eighties, I'm sure it was quite something for her to see a woman preaching the message or leading the church. Most recently, her mind was beginning to diminish, demonstrated by her ability to take walks and then not be quite sure how to return home, or have conversations that didn't fully make sense. But no one cared. She was a well-respected member of the church, and everyone loved her, including me.

Every Thursday morning, she faithfully attended a prayer meeting at the church. One morning, as all our eyes were closed, she commenced: "Dear God, please don't let us have a woman pastor. We will be an embarrassment to all the other churches." She said this out loud... sitting right beside me.

I opened my eyes. Two women sitting across the table from me opened their eyes. In disbelief. But this sweet lady continued with eyes closed, head bowed, in sincere conversation with her Creator.

No one said anything. We knew that at this point in her journey of dementia, she was simply parroting what she heard at home. And she prayed it every week, seemingly oblivious that it had anything to do with me.

Throw a pebble on the pile. I'm an embarrassment.

A year after our mental health retreat, the women of the church gathered at Cedar Springs Retreat Centre once again—our annual time to connect during a weekend away. On the Saturday evening while the women visited, played board games, and chatted away in the knitting corner, an elderly lady approached me. "I'm going to vote for you." She intended to show her support to me, but I needed to clear up her misconceptions about the bylaw change process happening at the church.

"This really isn't about me. The church is proposing that we change the bylaw regarding the lead pastor role, and if it's passed, then I will have the opportunity to apply for the job, just like all the other candidates. You are not voting for me; you are voting to change the bylaw." She smiled and gave my arm a friendly squeeze. I don't think I convinced her. The conversation with her unnerved me, as I wondered whom she had been talking to and why she felt she needed to let me know of her support.

Throw a pebble on the pile. People are taking sides. I'm causing division in the church.

A pastor whom I respected and always believed supported women at all levels of leadership shared some unsettling news with me. We were discussing the situation brewing at my church, and I encouraged him to speak up on behalf of women. He was a person of influence and diplomacy. I had known him for years and had assumed he would champion me. He chose his words carefully as he delicately broke the news to me: "I think it's only fair to tell you that I still hold to a complementarian [male-only leadership] viewpoint."

My stomach churned with disbelief. I hadn't expected this from him. As we talked, I tried to keep my facial expressions professional and not let my response come off as too emotional. But all I really wanted to do was scream, "Noooo!"

I confronted him. "How can you truly support me when you don't believe that women should be able to lead in any role?"

"My personal beliefs do not change my support for you. I assure you that I am open-minded and can support you as a lead pastor, even if, at present, my theology doesn't agree with it. Give me time. Remember, it took nine years for your lead pastor to make the ideological switch."

My heart broke. I appreciated his honesty and his openness to express that even though he wasn't there yet, his views on the topic might change in the future. He was being a friend to me the best way he could, but it scared me. Who else thought like him? How many others did I take for granted would defend equality for women in the church, but I assumed wrongly? It was a sad reminder that I never really knew who I could count on.

Throw another pebble on the pile. Being female in church leadership can be so lonely.

I had become accustomed to the low-level discriminations and exclusions I had experienced over the years and accepted it as part of the package of being a female leader. But there came a time in my church when the tide began to change. No longer was it a stroll on the beach with the occasional gust of wind pushing me aside. Watching where I walked to avoid a sharp shell or a crab that might nibble on my toe. The tide had come in all the way up to the breakwater, and the weather had become cold and stormy. I needed to be careful as I walked along the boardwalk lest I fall into the angry waters.

The Owners started to come after me personally. They might not be able to stop women from leadership roles in general, but they were certainly going to stop one woman from one role. And let's be clear here, at this point, I hadn't yet applied for the job.

Sunday mornings quickly transitioned into an invisible battleground, with a few people on the attack, a few in defence, and the majority completely oblivious to the tensions brewing. Typically after the Sunday morning service, I loved to greet people and chat with them about what was going on in their lives. Therefore, one Sunday, I was shocked when I offered my hand to an elderly gentleman (knew he wasn't a hugger), and he looked at me blankly, turned his back, and walked away. Was I missing something? This man had always been cordial to me. When I got home, I shared the incident with my husband, and he said the fellow did the same thing to him. We realized it was definitely a rebuke.

The following Sunday morning, a staff member was sitting at the back of the church in the sound booth. He was not visible to anyone else because of the computer monitors that obscured his presence. He overheard a congregant warn another that I was going to lead the church into apostasy; I would lead the church away from an orthodox understanding of the faith. I didn't realize I had such power. Maybe I should run for political office.

One of the worst moments during my time as interim lead pastor was when one of The Owners came to the church office when I wasn't there and attempted to persuade a staff member of my unsuitability for the job. He tried to convince my co-worker that seminary, the place where I got a master's degree in the study of our Christian faith, had ruined my mind and that I no longer loved God. I can imagine he longed for the days when women weren't even allowed to attend seminary. How come this accusation had never been lobbed at any of the male pastors I worked with? They had all studied at the same school as me. My co-worker's insistent defence of me was met with threats that this person's own job should be under reconsideration.

When this staff member told me what happened, it seemed like someone else's story. This couldn't really be happening. I wrote the words down in my daytimer: "Seminary ruined her mind. She no longer loves God." Over the next few weeks, I would stare at them and wallow in self-pity. I felt so betrayed. I knew some people felt strongly about the issue of female leadership. I was aware of the slander behind my back. I had been informed of the letters that were being written arguing against the proposed bylaw change. But I couldn't believe that people were actively trying to sabotage me.

I was doing a job I loved, serving a group of people I had known for over twenty years. They had shared their family heartbreaks and confided some of their greatest losses with me. They had witnessed my children grow up and lovingly spent time with them over the years. They thanked me for my teaching and shared how it impacted their lives. They appreciated the praise and support I gave them as they led ministries and did good works at the church. Nothing had changed on my part. The only thing that had changed was that I had the audacity to want to apply for a job they believed only a man should have.

The Owners weren't holding anything back.

Throw a boulder on the pile!

I received the distressing news that this issue was no longer isolated to our specific church. I was stunned to hear that churches halfway across the country would consider leaving the denomination if a woman became lead pastor at our church. Could I really be the source of a national controversy? What happened to our denomination's stance that every church can decide for themselves about these issues? Was the concept of a female pastor so offensive that they couldn't even tolerate it for others? These male leaders didn't even know me, but their contempt for the idea of women in leadership was so strong, they were ready to take drastic action.

Not my problem. Still, throw another pebble on the pile.

CHAPTER 15

If I Were a Man

If I had been born male, how different would my story have been? As I listened to Taylor Swift's 2019 song "The Man," I was surprised by my anger. My guilty pleasure was to play it on repeat, my headphones concealing that I was listening to the same song twenty times over. It didn't help my spiritual health or my emotional well-being to indulge myself this way, but I resonated with the song's message—life is easier if you're a guy. I was tired of how I was treated and how most men do not even realize they benefit from their male privilege.

Being a woman in leadership often feels like being at an unfair track meet. Men and women all line up at the starting point, side by side. The finish line is the same for everyone. But when the starting pistol sounds, someone runs out and places hurdles every ten metres on the women's lanes. The women can never move around the track as fast as the men.

I like being a woman and feel confident that God loves me exactly the way I am. But it was an emotional struggle when others—people I respected, those in authority—attempted to make me feel less than my male counterparts. The first time I was at a national event with the denomination, I went for lunch with a group of pastors. As we ate, one of the men took on the role of host, working his way around the table, inquiring about each person and their church. But he had no questions for me. His exclusion of me was so obvious that I was embarrassed for him because he lacked such tact. I sat at the table with the men, but he ensured my participation was limited. *We will tolerate your presence out of politeness, but don't expect that we will consider you one of us.*

When I became an elder and preached my first few sermons at my church, a woman approached me after the service. She shared how much she appreciated my Sunday morning messages, and with great enthusiasm and sincerity, she shared some encouragement: "You are a wonderful teacher." And then, just so I didn't get the wrong impression, she clarified, "You're not a preacher, but a very good teacher." I failed to respond to her immediately, mostly because I was trying to process what she was saying. She took this as her sign to repeat what she just told me. I nodded politely but couldn't bring myself to say thank you.

"You're a teacher, not a preacher." Why did she have to make that distinction? I was doing the same thing as the male preachers in the church. Was this her way of justifying her enjoyment of my sermons but also sticking by her theological leanings that women shouldn't preach? If we call it teaching, then what I do is allowable? Her words taunted me for months. Why was it so hard for her to concede that what I was doing was called preaching? I don't believe she would ever have said that to a man, even a young one just starting in his career.

A few years later, when I had become the associate pastor at my church, one of the denomination's leaders invited me to give a talk at a national event. I did a short teaching on contemplative prayer and then invited everyone present to join me in a prayer exercise. As I read the text, my eyes were open. Everyone else in the room had their heads bowed and eyes closed as they engaged in the prayer. Everybody, except one man. I couldn't believe it was happening again. Just like the man who showed his displeasure when I applied for the associate pastor role at my church, this man was sitting in the back row obviously disgruntled with the whole situation. His eyes didn't blink; his gaze never left my face. His arms were crossed, and his body was slumped in the chair like a toddler who refused to eat dinner. I had been invited to be there, so there wasn't much he could do about it, but he did a very good job conveying his discontent. For every man who would recognize my skills and abilities to lead, there'd be another to ensure I knew I didn't belong in this environment.

If I were a man, he and I could have become friends. We were about the same age, both in leadership, and cared passionately about the work of the denomination in Canada. Perhaps we would have had coffee together, discussing what I presented or having a rousing theological conversation about something else that had been presented at the conference that week. But no. I was a woman, and in his opinion, what I was doing was unacceptable.

But sometimes men like him surprised me. Even though they might not be kind to me, it doesn't mean they aren't caring individuals. One time when I was once again the only woman at a meeting, I witnessed such a scenario. It was time for a coffee break, and the cafeteria server who brought the drinks and snacks was having a difficult time negotiating the door and her food cart. One of the men jumped up and immediately ran to the other side of the room to help her. He held the door and inquired if there was anything else he could do. He profusely thanked her for bringing the refreshments. His gallantry was a bit over the top, I thought. I watched in amazement at this whole scene. It wasn't what he was doing that was remarkable, but who was doing it.

This man typically would not even speak to me. I knew that he was strongly opposed to women in even the lowest levels of leadership, so my presence was an offence to him. He would always respond if I addressed him, but he would never initiate a conversation with me. He certainly had never rendered an ounce of friendliness toward me, even though he appeared congenial with all the men, enjoying conversation and a good laugh with them. I had become used to this type of exclusion, but still, how can you dislike me when you've never gotten to know me?

Why was I so shocked when he acted kindly toward the cafeteria woman? It occurred to me that it was his way of affirming her. Here was a woman who was doing what she was supposed to. She wasn't at the table but serving those who gathered at it. It was the first time I was able to see him with different eyes. He probably was a loving husband and father. He likely was caring toward the women he pastored. As long as everyone knew their place.

The influence of the Christian church has been a contributor to the increasingly improved status of women, but it is also responsible for its history of patriarchy and its continued adherence to this view in many streams of Christianity. Throughout its history, the church's leading theologians and authors have referred to women as inferior, less intelligent, lacking in morals, and even "the devil's gateway"—famously spouted by second-century author Tertullian.[9] Many of these teachings are drawn from the Bible's creation story. A simplistic explanation: Adam, the man, was created before Eve, the woman. Eve ate the fruit before Adam. Therefore, man is the superior creature.

Even during the Enlightenment period of the eighteenth century, some scientists reasoned that women's smaller heads meant they possessed weaker brains. They asserted that women are biologically more like children, once again affirming the superiority of men.[10] It's an unconscious bias that permeates our

....

9   Frank Forrester Church, "Sex and Salvation in Tertullian," *Harvard Theological Review* 68, no.2 (April 1, 1975): 83–101.

10   Beth Allison Barr, *The Making of Biblical Womanhood: How the Subjugation of Women Became Gospel Truth* (Grand Rapids, MI: Brazos Press, 2021), 162.

culture even today. When my husband and I were on vacation, we decided to play chess in the cruise ship's lounge. I decided to brush off my middle school chess champion skills to teach my husband the game. A senior man walked by, and he stopped to observe us playing. He addressed my husband with a wink and a smile and said, "Teaching the little lady how to play, are we?" We nodded and smiled as we groaned on the inside.

We've moved past this, correct? These ridiculous notions of women being evil or less intelligent don't exist today, right? Women lead countries, are CEOs of companies, and are presidents of Ivy League universities. And yet the struggle to determine reasons for their inferiority persists.

In the twentieth century, within the church, the idea of women as inherently evil or less intelligent had been updated to women simply being more gullible. Women can't be trusted to teach or lead because look what silly little Eve did, being deceived into disobedience (never mind that today Christian scholars have varying viewpoints on the Adam and Eve story). How can women be trusted to lead when they are so easily fooled? I was provided this explanation many times in my early years of church leadership. It's so galling, it's hard to even respond.

More recently, as those in power realize that the sweeping generalization of women as gullible is incredibly offensive, there's been a move to replace gullibility with the claim that women are too emotional. It is just not politically correct these days to describe women as evil or stupid, but emotional is still acceptable. Important decisions, the teaching of doctrine, and the leading of people must be done by those who are not swayed by the unreliability of feelings. The job must be done by men. Unfortunately, this is why women in leadership feel the urge to act more like men. No tears. Stiff upper lip. Be direct. If being accused of being emotional is a disqualifying attribute, then emotions in public must be suppressed.

One time in a staff meeting, a female colleague became upset, and the tears started to flow. She immediately apologized for her behaviour. I responded by sharing about a study I had recently read that claimed that women's tears aren't just shed in sorrow but when they are extremely angry. In leadership, anger is generally accepted as an appropriate emotion. Sadness isn't. This research on women's emotions made her feel better about crying. And I also felt better about my own tears. I knew that the times I had shed them at work were not from a position of weakness but from an anger that was stirred by the injustice and seemingly hopelessness of my situation. Women are not less competent because they are sensitive or relational; instead, this is their superpower. I know many men who are very relational, and this is the key quality that makes them wonderful pastors.

Despite what I knew to be true, all these ideas, whether spoken or unspoken, affected how I presented and shared ideas when I was in a room full of men. I never knew if my contribution to the discussion or theology debate was discounted because there was an underlying belief by some that I was inherently less discerning than my peers. Did they think that my intrinsic gullibility allowed them to question even my wisest contributions? Even when I felt respected in a room, I never knew with certainty who was fully accepting of me. The men in the room who are fully supportive of women are hesitant to speak up because they don't want to offend the pastors who believe in male-only leadership. And the men who do believe that women should only participate in a supportive role in the church often don't speak their minds because of the pushback they will get from their more progressive counterparts. So we all converse, discuss, and plan, politely keeping our fears and biases to ourselves.

Fortunately, life surprises us with occasions to forget our prejudices. The two world wars of the twentieth century created opportunities for women. With many of the men away at war, the women left the sphere of being homemakers and entered the workforce, but many were forced to give up their jobs when the men returned. I've even heard that our denomination had a female lead pastor at a church in Alberta in the early 1940s. I don't know anything about her, but I wonder if she was able to lead her church because there was no man to do so. Did she have to stop when the war was over? No one wishes for a crisis, but it is often in these times that we can look past our small-minded prejudices and just allow the best person for the job to step up to the plate.

Within my lifetime, I've seen some interesting changes as well. As a child, I recall my mother signing her cheques by adding "Mrs." in front of my father's full name. She did not use her first name but identified as the feminized version of my father. In our thirty-two years of marriage, my husband has consistently pushed back on practices like this. He's always made sure my name is first on documents such as real estate contracts and banking papers. Every time he ordered more cheques from the bank (back when we used them), he put my name first on the request. And every single time we received them, his name took top billing. The bank always did us the favour of ensuring the man's name came first—*like it should be.*

Men as leaders is still the default setting for many churches. A random look at many church websites reveals that most of the pastors and elders are men. That is slowly changing in many churches, and it's aided by men who have started taking down some of those hurdles on the racetrack that slow women down—sometimes in the smallest of ways.

Typically when I'm at a conference or a denominational gathering, the speakers always use the pronoun "he" when referring to pastors. When 95 per cent of the pastors in the room are male, it's easy to understand why. But occasionally, a man will give a presentation and intentionally uses "she" as well as "he" when referring to pastors. It's such a gift of inclusion. Trust me, every woman in the room notices. How wonderful to use both pronouns together. Recognizing both the men and women working together in the church.

Like it should be.

CHAPTER 16

Norms

That's statistically impossible! I screamed in my head. During a meeting with other church leaders, the topic of women in leadership came up. A pastor from another church offered, "I believe in having women in leadership positions, but unfortunately, in our church, we've never had a woman who has demonstrated leadership potential." He seemed genuinely saddened by this supposed fact.

I was flabbergasted, especially because I knew some of the women from his church, the one he had led for over twenty-five years. They had even attended our Women in Leadership conference. I don't care where you work or play—it is impossible that no woman has ever had the potential to be a leader in your environment. It's circular thinking. We have no women leaders because we have no women with leadership skills... *because you have no women leaders!*

Who is mentoring the young women in your church? Have you ever had a female guest speaker? What opportunities are they given? Can the women in your church even imagine themselves in leadership roles? If there has not been one woman who is suitable for leadership in all that time, this means you have a patriarchal culture that does not instruct and prepare women to develop into these roles. The sad thing is that I believe this fellow was being sincere. He seemed truly disappointed there were no potential female leaders in his midst.

When I was a child, the patriarchal system of my church was the "norm"—what seemed proper and normal to everyone involved—and did not challenge my conscience until the day I saw my mother washing communion cups in the church kitchen. The men were the pastors and leaders. That's just the way it was.

My parents held traditional roles in the family, my father being the breadwinner as a math and science teacher and my mother taking care of my brother, sister, and me at home. Typical of her generation, her nursing degree was only to provide for her until she had children. Even though they worked within a traditional framework, I never had a sense that was expected of me. I grew up to be a confident female and felt their permission to follow any path I would choose.

When I entered grade eleven, my best friend suggested we apply for the Rotary Exchange Program, and the two of us imagined what sophisticates we'd be, living far away in another country. I was thrilled to be chosen to live in Belgium for my grade twelve year. Another girl (not my best friend) was chosen to go to Sweden, and every month in preparation for our trips, we would join the Rotary group for lunch. We would give updates about our exchange plans and get to know the men who were sponsoring us. There we were, two seventeen-year-old girls, regularly having lunch with eighty men.

When I arrived in Belgium, the same pattern was repeated. My sponsoring club in Charleroi hosted five girls from different parts of the world, and once a month, we'd have lunch at the club, each girl seated at a table with seven men. It did feel awkward at times being both young and female in their midst, but what's interesting about "norms" is that I perceived it as just that—normal. I was not offended to be there but felt honoured. I didn't question the absence of female Rotary members because everyone knew that Rotary was a men's club. Why would women be there?

Although I was not asking that question at the time, there must have been many women older than me who were having those discussions. Even though Rotary is considered a service club, not a social club, it was certainly the place in most towns where networking and business connections were made. The women who were burdened by this exclusion fought to have it changed, because within a few years of my exchange, the prohibition was lifted and women could join Rotary clubs anywhere in the world.

Norm violations often make people uncomfortable. If something has been done one way for many years, it's considered the accurate or most truthful way. Norms make people feel safe, that life is proceeding as it should. Women in leadership positions are often viewed as norm violations because they are so often underrepresented in these roles. Therefore, when they present themselves in these situations, it is natural for people to have strong negative reactions.[11]

It is through personal experience that I've realized that it isn't well-presented arguments that change people's minds. And I certainly tried. I knew the points of discussion on both sides of the issue, and I would gift well-written books on the topic to those who struggled to accept that women could lead at all levels of the church. But those strategies had little effect.

The best persuaders were time and persistence. As the years ticked by and people got used to seeing me lead, it became more normative for them. One Sunday, in the back row of pews in the church, I sat with a sixty-year-old woman who I knew held conservative views. She leaned over to me and, in not much more

11   Caroline Criado Perez, *Invisible Women: Data Bias in a World Designed for Men* (New York, NY: Abrams Press, 2019), 267.

than a whisper, said, "I have never believed that a woman should lead a church, but you've changed that for me."

Contrasting this reaction was a young woman who had recently started attending the church. Smart, dynamic, confident. She shared with a staff member that she liked what I had done for women in our church, and in principle, she believed a woman could be a lead pastor. But… she'd rather have a man. She said it just felt more "normal."

When discussing the topic of women in church leadership, one of the most frustrating conversations I had was when a male pastor kindly mansplained to me, "We just have to do what is best for the majority." I looked around the room and realized that I was the only woman there. He was trying to reason with me that decisions needed to be made about what would work best for most people. *Most* meaning men. So how will things ever change if all the men are in charge and they make up the majority? How will equality ever arrive when those deciding on change only represent half the population?

When I think of the mission of the church, shouldn't the attitude be one of "all hands on deck"? Regardless of whether one is male or female, extrovert or introvert, academic or humanitarian, teacher or counsellor, wouldn't you want everyone contributing their strengths toward the mission? And if the one who has the greatest influence on the group is a woman, shouldn't we allow her to use that strength? If the one who inspires the crowd to a vision is a man with a poetic soul rather than academic fortitude, shouldn't he be able to guide the group? Why does the leader need to be the person who is the most vocal or assertive? Maybe we need to listen more to the whispered wisdom rather than the charismatic call.

I have witnessed the intuitiveness of women who have had solutions that didn't align with the consensus of the male majority. When they made suggestions, those ideas were overlooked, only to be considered when nothing else worked. When their proposal eventually proved successful, they were not even credited. So much time had passed, and no one remembered whom the idea came from. It is my experience (which may not be universal) that in meetings, women often wait their turn to speak, and some only comment when given a direct invitation to do so. I have had to encourage many women to speak up at church meetings, assuring them that their ideas are just as valuable as men's.

Why is it that our world has taken a "male-first" way of living? Men have always been included in every aspect of life: sports, education, politics, and every type of work. Why have women had to earn the right to participate?

I'm not a scholar in history or theology, but I can make my best educated guess—because people think God is a man. You might argue that it only affects the religious world, but until recent history, everybody participated in some form of religion, and it influenced every aspect of one's life.

Power isn't necessarily a bad thing. It's only when it's corrupted that it evolves into control. The people living in Palestine in Jesus's day had been waiting for God to rescue them from the oppression of living under Roman rule. When Jesus claimed to be God, some embraced him because they believed he would use his power to free them from their enemies. But Rabbi Jesus came to teach and model a different kind of power—love. He taught a message of peace, loving your enemies, and taking care of the poor and sick. Some accepted his teaching and became his followers, but many others were upset that Jesus wouldn't get political and get rid of their oppressors. And so they killed him. (Christians believe he was raised from the dead three days later.) Over two thousand years later, those who claim to follow the way of Jesus still struggle with the tug of war of power versus love.

What if God had come as a woman when he put the human jumpsuit on? Would she have been able to convey the message of God's character and love to people? I don't think so. She wouldn't have been given an education or allowed in the temple to teach. She couldn't have just headed out with twelve of her gal pals (at least six of whom would have been named Mary) to go and share about God's love for people. She couldn't have left home, period. She would have been too busy taking care of her husband and children. God probably came as a man because no one would have listened if he had been a woman. The message Jesus conveyed is believed (even though not always put into practice well) by billions of people today. If he came as a woman, no one would have heard anything.

Due to the ingrained patriarchy of the day, God needed to come to earth as a "he." But if you want to refer to God as "she," go right ahead. There's a lot of discussion around pronouns today, but using them limits who God is and how he relates to us. I can't bring myself to describe him as "it," so for simplicity's sake, I'll stick with the male pronoun that everyone is accustomed to.

There's a famous piece of art by Dutch painter Rembrandt (that's his first name, who knew?) from the seventeenth century called *The Return of the Prodigal Son*. It's based on the story of the same name in the Bible.[12] A son from the ancient world asks his father for an advance on his inheritance and then takes off and spends it all on wild living. Eventually, when he no longer has any money, food, or friends, he decides to return home and beg his father to allow him back to be a servant in the household. He feels the great weight of shame, but when his father sees him, he is so overjoyed at his return that he has a giant party for his son. In short, it's a metaphor for how God is always ready to welcome us home.

Go to the computer and ask Ms. Google to show you the painting. In this teaching story that Jesus told, the father

....

12   Luke 15:11–32 (NIV).

represents God. But look at the father's hands. They are different. One hand is large and masculine, and the other is smaller and more feminine in appearance. Rembrandt used his art to depict God giving both fatherly and motherly love. Subtle and beautiful.

One day, a friend and I were attending an event at the church, and we watched a video that showed this story with a female protagonist in a modern setting. A Prodigal Daughter. She heads off to the big city where she makes a terrible wreck of her life. When she returns home, her father welcomes her with open arms. I didn't find the video that rousing. *Yeah. Yeah. I know this story*, I thought to myself, possessing the impatience that comes with overfamiliarity with the narrative. But my friend had a completely different reaction: "This is the first time I've understood this story. God loves me even though I've really messed up my life."

To be honest, I was quite surprised. It was the exact same story except that the main character was a woman instead of a man. But that just shows the power of representation. People need to see themselves in a story.

CHAPTER 17
Heretic

As the tensions within the church began to build, I implored the board to do something. They weren't just the spiritual leaders of the church; they were also my employer. Churches like to view themselves as a family, which is good. But under Canadian law, they are also an employer and subject to employment laws. When I was an X-ray technologist, we had strict policies regarding harassment. We were protected from bullying from our colleagues, the doctors, and even the patients. I'm sorry, no, the customer is not always right. They certainly don't have the right to abuse the staff, and my boss was always quick to mediate and defend us in difficult situations.

The difference is that at a church, the "customer" is also a member of the family. To defend me means having to give tough love to another family member. The Owners had been at the church longer than I had. They'd been involved and generous with their time and money for many years. So even though it was apparent to everyone that they were acting horribly, the elders hesitated to do anything about it. Surely things will just calm down on their own.

Our church leadership had always prided ourselves on two things about our church family: our people were very generous with their time and money, and we had a history of being a church without conflict. When I heard stories from other pastors about the friction on their boards, the disputes among staff, or the difficulties caused by church members, I was always so thankful for the harmony in my home church. But had all these years of smooth sailing not prepared us for the difficulties we were presently navigating?

John wanted to get a lawyer, as he'd reached his limit of tolerating the abuse directed at his wife. I think he was just speaking as an angry husband coming to my defence, but he'll argue that he did, in fact, want a lawyer, but never for a moment did I ever consider suing my church. It's interesting, though, because I'd likely not have the same hesitation if I was working in another field. What is it about working at a church that makes you feel that you can't fight for your rights, for the ability to work in an environment that is free from harassment?

In the fall of 2019, six months after I became the interim pastor, the conflict at the church was at its peak. Nevertheless, I was excited about a new sermon series I was about to present. For six weeks, I was going to explore different views on some Christian doctrines. Over the last 150 years in North America, there's been a growing fundamentalism that dictates there's only one understanding of certain beliefs. It arose in part as pushback to Charles Darwin's 1859 publication *Origin of the Species* and scholarly German higher criticism that questioned the historicity of many biblical accounts.[13] North American churches under the evangelical label felt the need to present a united front about their beliefs so that their adherents could *know with certainty* what they should believe. Christians started to embrace empiricism, claiming to bring a scientific certainty to the Bible that it was never meant to have. Never mind that science is not equated with

....

13   George M. Marsden. *Understanding Fundamentalism and Evangelicalism* (Eerdmans Publishing: Grand Rapids Michigan 1991), 12.

certainty, as scientists are always making new hypotheses to challenge what they know. Just as what we understand scientifically changes, so does our theology grow as we learn more about our universe and the world we live in. Galileo Galilei, the sixteenth-century astronomer, was threatened with excommunication from the church for his assertion that the earth circled the sun and not the other way around. Information that was received with horror five hundred years ago is ubiquitously accepted today.

As the Christian church enters the twenty-first century, there is a growing interest and acceptance of a variety of viewpoints within Christian theology. These teachings aren't new but have been discussed and debated throughout two thousand years of Christian history. People who are serious about their faith want to know why they believe what they do and understand why others in the faith believe differently. My goal with the sermon series was to simply share these varying viewpoints so that when our congregants met other Christians who thought differently than them, they wouldn't discount what they believed. Or, possibly, they could even learn from them.

Each week, I was going to present three positions on a topic, explain them, and provide some biblical and scholarly support for each. It wasn't my goal to persuade anyone of one specific view or even share my position on each doctrine. It was about simply introducing varying viewpoints and inviting us all into the exercise of critical thinking. It was time to step out of the echo chamber of "there is only one way to think about things."

For example, one lesson was going to be about the concept of hell. Some people believe there is a literal place where people are sent to be tormented for eternity. Others think that if you have chosen to live a life without God, you will be judged and cease to exist afterwards—annihilation. And still others believe that the love of God is greater than our resistance to him, and eventually all humans will be united with him.

The following Sunday's message would be about creation. Some believe God created the world six thousand years ago in six literal days. Others believe that the earth is very old. And still others believe that God used the evolutionary process in his creation. Once again, it wasn't about concluding which theory was correct; it was about learning together how different people interpret the creation narrative in the Bible. The bottom line is that all Christians believe that God created the cosmos (and continues to do so); we just differ on his method.

Before teaching on any of those subjects, I presented an introductory sermon. It was important to talk about heresy, a word that religious people have used for thousands of years when accusing others of inaccurate beliefs. During times when the passions of the religious world and the power of the political world were inextricably intertwined, bad things happened to heretics. I shared some examples:

In the Christian world, the sacrament of baptism is very important, a practice that indicates one's dedication to following the ways of Jesus Christ. In the Bible stories, this was most often done by immersing a person fully into a body of water. But within two hundred years after the Christian church began, the practice morphed. The primary mode of baptism became a priest sprinkling water on one's head, usually while still an infant. It wasn't until the 1500s that a European group called the Anabaptists proposed that believers should be baptized when they were old enough to understand the decision they were making, and it should be done by full immersion. The Christian church at the time was horrified, and do you know what they did to the Anabaptists? *You want full immersion; we'll give you full immersion!* And they drowned them for this heresy.[14]

14   "Zwingli's Persecution of the Anabaptist," World History Encyclopedia, accessed May 18, 2022, https://www.worldhistory.org/article/1932/zwinglis-persecution-of-the-anabaptists.

The second example I presented was of William Tyndale. He was a sixteenth-century British priest who could speak seven languages plus ancient Hebrew and Greek (two of the languages of the original texts of the Bible). He translated the Bible into English, believing that its message was one that everyone should be able to read in their own language. It was illegal to do this in England because the church leaders insisted that the Bible must be read in the original languages. Therefore, Tyndale produced the English Bibles in Germany and smuggled them back into his home country. King Henry VIII and the church leaders declared him "the captain of English heretics" and feared that if people were able to read the Bible in their mother tongue, chaos would ensue.[15] So he was condemned as a heretic, stripped of his priesthood, strangled to death, and his body burned at the stake. It was Tyndale's translations that eventually greatly contributed to the production of the King James Bible.

In more recent times, some seminary professors have lost their jobs because they no longer adhere to the regimented list of what they must exactly believe to teach at their institutions. I know of pastors who have either lost their positions or never gotten a job because they differed from the church's statement of faith over one doctrine. And we have endless divisions within the Protestant Church, resulting in thousands of different denominations because people aren't willing to hold space for different views than their own. Instead, we pick up our ball (our pew, our pulpit) and go play elsewhere. How can it be that every different Christian church has the right way to think?

This fundamentalism, this desire to be certain of all the great mysteries of God and his ways, comes from fear. How will I know what God wants? How will I know how to live? I need

....

15 Steven. J. Lawson, *The Daring Mission of William Tyndale* (Sanford, FL: Reformation Trust Publishing, 2015), 9, 17, Kindle.

a checklist of everything that Christians should believe. I need to understand the right way so I don't make any mistakes. Jesus made it quite clear that the most important command is to love God and love other people. Ironically, so many people ignore this instruction as they fight for things of lesser importance.

Today, Christian churches no longer have a problem with reading an English Bible. That just makes sense if it's your primary language. Each church also respects the other's opinions on modes of baptism. One church might not agree with the other regarding baptism, but they wouldn't call each other heretics. Why? Because we are slowly becoming less dogmatic and learning to become more gracious with whom we don't agree. We are starting to recognize that some of our viewpoints are moulded by our traditions, cultural expectations, and denominational backgrounds. When I was a child, I was taught that certain Christian churches weren't even Christian because they didn't do things like our church did. I no longer believe that. And most of my contemporaries who grew up in the church don't either. Humility teaches us that our ways aren't always *the* ways. Our theology changes as we participate in communal critical thinking. My introductory sermon was preparing the people for the sermon series in the weeks ahead. They were about to hear some theology that was new to them, that they had no context for—that they might have a visceral reaction to.

After a service on a Sunday morning, feedback is inevitable. One man in his thirties shared that if he had heard a sermon like this in his teenage years, he would have never left the church (only to return to it recently). Like many others, he stopped attending church as a teenager when confronted with the ultimatum that one must believe in certain ideas or you couldn't call yourself a Christian.

Many members of the church expressed appreciation for the conversations we were about to have. An older couple visiting the church shared that it was the best sermon they had heard in years. People made suggestions of subjects they'd like me to explore.

A positive buzz was brewing.

Then I went out to the church lobby.

I could see one of The Owners talking to an elder and she didn't look happy. In the moment, it didn't concern me greatly. Not everyone will agree with everything you say on a Sunday morning. People are allowed to discuss their thoughts about the message with each other. But as I said goodbye to another congregant, I saw her coming my way. She walked directly toward me, and I presumed that we were about to have a difficult conversation. She kept her voice low so as not to make a scene in front of the other church members, who were sipping their coffee and catching up with friends.

She began speaking, poised and self-controlled, but soon lost her restraint. My introductory sermon had upset her, and her objections were hurled my way with no opportunity for me to respond. "How can you preach a sermon series like that? These are things I have believed since I was a child. You are mocking my beliefs. You are going to ruin our church. You are part of the 'great deception' that will lead Christians into apostasy."

I stood there awestruck at the irony of our exchange. After the sermon I just preached, she basically called me a heretic. Even though I just finished explaining to the whole church how we so wrongly accuse others of this.

Her anger prevented any reasonable conversation, but I did try. I assured her that I was going to teach on multiple viewpoints, including her own. I was going to present various ways of understanding certain doctrines, rather than insisting on what I believed. But I guess she was scared. Afraid that I might attempt to disassemble her belief system. So she kept repeating her concerns.

In a moment of what I considered inspiration, especially in such a stressful situation, I pivoted the conversation. As gently as I could, because I knew how agitated she was, I said, "Most of the viewpoints I hold are no different than what Pastor Chris believes." I aligned myself doctrinally with the previous pastor, whom I knew she respected. I wanted her to understand that I wasn't off on some heretical path, hoping to lead everyone in the room theologically astray. This information stunned her a bit, but her next move was to suddenly turn and march defiantly out the front doors of the church.

I stared at the front entrance for a while. Was this the woman who used to greet me with such charm and warmth each Sunday? Had the issue of women and church leadership created such turmoil for her that she could no longer trust me? If Pastor Chris had given the same sermon that I had just presented, would she have responded to him this way?

In hindsight, I was naïve about the grip fundamentalism (black-and-white thinking, no capacity to consider other viewpoints) had in our church. I was used to working with a staff team that was able to have open-minded conversations on topics, even when we didn't all agree. Perhaps they weren't a good test market for these subjects because they were excited to learn new things. I never imagined that this sermon series would cause certain people such angst.

It would have been better had I first preached a sermon series on how to disagree well or what the inclusive love of God could mean, but I didn't appreciate how necessary that was. These topics had never been discussed in this way, and some people weren't ready to be stripped of their certainty that there was only one way to think. They didn't agree with me that we needed to talk about the things that no one was talking about.

Good thing church and state are no longer joined at the hip. No one had the authority to drown, burn, or imprison me.

CHAPTER 18
Critical Thinking

I called it a gift. My sermon that day was a gift to The Owners. Beautifully wrapped, topped with a bow, presented on a platter. Ammunition against me that had nothing to do with my gender. They had been working hard to prevent the proposed bylaw change, and attacking me was now part of the process. But it's hard when the main accusation is that I am the wrong gender. It's difficult to be openly discriminatory, even when you feel that religious freedom gives you that right. But finally, they had something much more politically correct to use against me.

I was a false teacher.

No longer was it necessary to say, *This woman can't lead us*; now they could say, *This person can't lead us. She will teach us incorrect doctrine. She will ruin the church.*

The funny thing was that I hadn't taught on anything yet. My introductory lesson simply explained that in the upcoming weeks, we were going learn about some alternative ways of viewing certain Christian doctrines. If we *know* something to be true, then there is little attempt to do any critical thinking about it. But when we start to appreciate that there are differing views on important topics, we can give them some intellectual consideration.

The Owners went right to the board with their protest.

Unaware of how much fuel I had added to the fire, I went home that Sunday afternoon with a strange juxtaposition of feelings: elation and dread. I was proud of following through on my vision to introduce critical thinking on a variety of topics. This was going to be something new for our church. I was eager to hear about the conversations people would have in their weekly home groups, discussing questions on each topic. I had carefully selected books that would go in our church library so people could continue to study on their own. Excitement welled up in me as I looked forward to presenting the rest of the series.

But I also said to my husband that afternoon, "That might have been my very last sermon." My Spidey senses were tingling, warning that there may be some danger ahead. And yet I was at peace. I had been invited to lead the church, not babysit it. Most of the church was enthusiastically looking forward to the following weeks' messages, but I had a sense that for some, I had rattled their cozy echo chamber a little too much. That had certainly not been my intent. I wasn't young and brash or possessed an attitude of "you're going to learn new things whether you like it or not." I knew that effective change often must be approached slowly and by simply starting conversations. That's what I thought I was doing.

The phone call came the following day. A couple of the elders wanted to meet with me.

I don't think any of us were looking forward to that meeting, but a couple of days later, the three of us gathered in my office at the church. I had always been on good terms with both these men, so our conversation was civil yet intense. They expressed surprise over the content of my sermon, and I reminded them that I had shared an outline of the whole sermon series with them at the previous board meeting. They had only a vague recollection of that. I found that odd because I had presented it with such enthusiasm.

Their big concern was why I had to present that content on a Sunday morning. *Couldn't I have just had a class on a weekday evening, and those who were interested could attend? Had I really thought it wise to present that content to the entire congregation?* I argued that leadership often involves taking people where they don't even know they need to go. Why have a class with only a handful of people when this was teaching the whole church needed? (At the time, this may have seemed to be newer ground to break, but in 2024, these conversations are happening every-where—in churches, books, and many podcasts.) As they dispensed their questions and concerns, I could feel the frustration in me welling up. *We can't cater to fear. We have each been elected by this church to lead and guide the people who have chosen us to do so.*

I understood their predicament. They were being respectful of the invitation they extended to me to lead the church, but they also had to deal with members of the congregation. And at this time, The Owners' voices were much louder, spiraling out of control with doses of fear and anger. As my conversation with the two elders continued, I felt like someone had punched me in the gut; my body was indicating its awareness that so much of what I was enjoying in my life at present was soon going to come to an end. I had worked so hard to get there and couldn't believe that it might all be over. I kept my composure, but even the fingernails dug into the back of my hand couldn't stop the tears that were stinging my eyes. Fortunately, none ran down my face as I tried to remain calm.

Sensing that my time at this church was likely going to end, I posed a question to them both, because if I didn't ask it, I'd always be curious about it. I asked them if they could perceive me as a lead pastor or had they only ever envisioned me as the interim. One nodded affirmatively, indicating his support of me in the lead role. The other, the man whose opinion of me I was more unsure of, quietly said, "Yes, over these past seven months,

I've come to see the potential of you becoming the lead pastor—except for one occasion."

He had my attention. And he continued with his explanation. "There was just that one time when you inserted yourself into a conversation that had nothing to do with you." He was referring to the awful night of the board meeting when they discussed who the interim pastor might be and I had to speak up for myself. He gave me an honest answer, so I didn't dispute him. The embarrassment of that awful evening still hung over me as well. Afterwards, I couldn't help thinking that if I hadn't spoken up for myself, he would never have had the opportunity to see me in the role. His perception of me had changed because he had seen me do the job. I found it interesting that he felt it distasteful that I had "inserted myself into the conversation," but it was that exact action that allowed me to demonstrate to him that I was capable in that position.

No decision was made on that day. They weren't going to tell me to discontinue the sermon series, but they made their opinion clear that they didn't think it would be wise to do so. I needed time to think. I told them that if I abandoned the series and preached on a different topic the following Sunday, they should take that as a sign that I've concluded that this church is not the place for me. I wanted to lead the church I cared for so dearly, but I knew I couldn't work in an environment where I was not free to lead as I saw best. They had to wait until Sunday to see what I would do.

That week, I did something I had never done before. On the Friday, I ditched my prepared sermon on the different views of hell and wrote a new complete sermon in one day. A nice safe one from Proverbs, the book of wisdom.

CHAPTER 19
He's Never Going to Marry You

Despite the elders' recent visit, there was no clarity to anyone, including me, about what was going on. None of the elders commented to me about my decision to not continue with the sermon series. Most of the congregation thought I had skipped a week in the series because it was Canadian Thanksgiving, and that I'd continue with the series the following week. I didn't want to act rashly, knowing that in a few weeks, the provincial denominational leader was coming to present teaching on the topic of women in leadership. And who knows what positive momentum that might provide.

That week, I just needed a mental break from it all. I love to read and decided I would find a book that would distract me from everything going on. So I ordered a book on my Kindle app. I love using e-books both on my phone and iPad and relish that there's little to no time between desiring a book and owning it. My husband has commented that perhaps I need a book budget. Ha! I'd like to see him try.

I bought a book called *Thirst* by Scott Harrison and spent the evening getting lost in the story of this New York party fiend extraordinaire. Through a radical personal transformation, his priorities changed, and he became passionate about providing clean water to communities in developing nations. His incredible journey helped me forget the pain of potentially losing something I had worked toward for so many years. It was good to get lost in such a fascinating story and have my mind on something other than the drama in my own life.

Deep into the story, I was sitting on my living room couch and looked up for a moment to stare out the window. And then I heard, *"He's never going to marry you."* What?! *"He's never going to marry you."* Was it the thoughts of my deep unconscious mind? Was it God speaking some sort of truth to me? Either way, I knew instantly what the "voice" was saying. Like a couple who lives together, and the woman desires marriage and the man doesn't, the "voice" was telling me that my church liked me enough to have me stay and work with it, but *it was never going to marry me.*

For fifteen years, I had served in leadership there, and many times, I wondered if I should stay. Leaving never seemed an option because this was my "home" and I had assignments here—people to love, teachings to share, help to give to the community. Yes, there were many challenges in being female clergy, but they were peppered among all the truly wonderful times. The pile of pebbles was always sitting off to the side, but most often, I was too busy and engaged in my work to think about it.

The Owners of the church caused me a significant amount of pain, but they weren't the ones who hurt me the most. They wouldn't have had the opportunity to do what they did if our church didn't already exist in an environment of disguised misogyny, extending from the national level down to the local churches. It might seem harsh to use the word *misogyny* because we equate it with hate, but its simple definition is "ingrained prejudice against women." It includes discreet microaggressions and overt exclusions. Sexist comments and a lack of job opportunities. The normalization of men always being in charge. It's not always acknowledged because it can be subtle, and many have grown accustomed to it and don't even realize it's happening. If you're not aware of it, then your misogyny radar probably hasn't been developed. But now, it was out in plain view, and no one was doing anything about it.

Instead of joining me in the fight against misogyny, I heard:

"You just need tougher skin." *My skin feels like leather.*

"Don't be too pushy; things will happen in God's time." *What if "God's time" is now? I think he's waiting for us to treat each other equally. But this is not a fight I can manage on my own.*

"Hold on, Michelle. You just need to stick with it." *This isn't just a bump in the road. I've been on the difficult path for years, and now I'm on the edge of a cliff. Your words of encouragement just make me feel weak and misunderstood. The subtext of your words implies a man would have the strength and perseverance to get through this.*

"I don't want to deal with the conflict. It's too messy." *You think it doesn't have anything to do with you, but you all have mothers, sisters, daughters, and female friends. And it affects them.*

A few weeks after I preached *that* sermon, the board met with provincial and national leadership. On the morning before they all met, our provincial leader presented a message on the theological supports for women in church leadership, followed by a Q&A session. Surely people would respond to this highly educated and well-respected leader. I excused myself from the meeting so that everyone could freely discuss the topic. The reports that trickled back to me afterwards indicated that most people had no questions on the topic, and that the queries presented to this leader were from the same few people who had been protesting all along. The morning session only seemed to aggravate the dissenters rather than bring clarity or peace to the situation.

After the morning service, the church board met with the provincial district minister and the national executive director to discuss the ongoing and increasingly tense issue that was gripping our church. I went home and had lunch, waiting to hear what decisions would be made.

I received a phone call. A couple of elders would like to meet with me. Again. This time, it was two different board members, both whom I respected, and one was a dear friend. It must have been so hard for her to remove her friend hat temporarily and put on her elder hat. We met the following day. The church was always closed on Mondays, so it offered us the privacy we needed. I sat and waited for them in the quiet of my church office, wondering how this meeting was going to affect the direction of my life. They were going to let me know what the board had decided.

They had wisely written out their thoughts in a letter. As I listened to it being read, I mentally agreed that what the board had decided was very good. It was what the church needed at this time. This time, there were no tears; I remained calm and unruffled. My friend later told me that she could read me and knew exactly what I was going to do. This surprised me because I thought I had been sporting my best poker face.

I went home and wrote my resignation letter.

Had they asked me to resign? Absolutely not. The plan was to bring in a transitional pastor, someone who specialized in helping churches navigate difficult situations. The board was clear that they wanted me to stay in my role as associate pastor, not only to assist the transitional pastor but to provide the church with some consistency in leadership. Someone else would lead the church through the process of the proposed bylaw change and he would need my help. They didn't know who it was going to be yet, but without a doubt, it would be a "he."

I couldn't stay. I knew the church was "never going to marry me," and for there to be any positive change around the issue of women in leadership, I needed to remove myself from the situation. I had become the lightning rod for everyone's angst on the issue. Others did not agree. "No, Michelle, you are tougher than this." "Your decision is disappointing." "We want you to stay." I wasn't a quitter and never have been. I had worked too hard for many years to simply walk away. I just knew that staying would not aid the process the church was about to go through.

My husband and I decided that I would give a month's notice, but then John proposed something that hadn't occurred to me. He suggested I remain for the next month to prepare the staff and organize everything for the transitional pastor but no longer attend Sunday morning services. I was surprised by this idea, but he'd had enough. "How are people supposed to know how serious this is if you just keep showing up with a smile on your face every week?" I knew what he was saying because it happens at most churches when a pastor leaves. The departure is always poised as a positive event. He or she is off to a new opportunity elsewhere. The awkward details of their firing or resignation are rarely revealed.

John and I had been careful not to share about the hurtful events or the actions of The Owners to people in the congregation. It wasn't just about avoiding gossip but recognizing that I was still the pastor of The Owners and I owed them a degree of care too. We hoped that our sudden absence on Sunday mornings would relate the message that something terrible must have happened for us to not even come to the worship services anymore. Even though we weren't telling the whole story, this provided the church family with a bit more transparency.

The board was disappointed with my decision, but they understood. As my friends, we had enjoyed visioning together and spending time with each other's families. As my employer, they had provided many opportunities for me and compensated me fairly. But this issue had become a monster that no one seemed to know how to subdue. I knew they planned on informing the church the following Sunday, so I needed to make a few house calls. I wanted some people to hear the news from me, not as a surprise on a Sunday morning.

I sat in the living room of a couple whom I had known for over twenty years. Our children grew up together. They welcomed me graciously into their home, and I shared that I would be leaving the church. They expressed their sorrow upon hearing my news, as they valued our friendship and the years we had spent together. I knew that they were conservative in many of their views, yet it still caught me off guard when they expressed that as much as they were sorry that I was leaving, "Men really need a man to lead them." The subtext of their comments was *What can we do? As much as we like you, you're not a man.* Sigh. No tears. Just a deep sadness. But this couple also gave me a gift. We disagreed on something pretty important to both parties but never were they mean. They are a fine example of how to disagree with someone and yet be kind.

I wasn't in church that Sunday when they made the announcement. Instead, I went for a long walk. I strolled through a cemetery, one that was close to my home but through which I had never ventured. I saw an elderly man sitting in a lawn chair by a headstone. I hesitated at first but eventually approached him because he looked so sad. We chatted for a while, and he told me stories of his deceased wife. Dave told me there was no longer any purpose to his life, and he came here every day to talk to her. We prayed together. We both were grieving great losses.

CHAPTER 20
Journey at Rivendell

It wasn't just the loss of a job. I lost my community of twenty-three years. These were the people my husband and I saw each week. We raised our children with them, went camping together, and celebrated each other's special milestones. Each year ticked off the annual events that bonded us: summer camps, September's Kick-off BBQs, Christmas Eve candlelight services (yes, real candles in small children's hands), and, of course, the highlight of the Christian calendar—celebrating Easter. Other people had told me that when they left their churches, grieving the loss of community was the hardest part, and I was about to experience it. My church family had been my tribe, and now that no longer existed. The people who were a consistent weekly presence in my life were gone (or so I thought at that moment).

I also knew that my career was over. That might seem like an overly dramatic claim, but I realized that I wouldn't be able to get a job in another church like the one I had. Most churches in my denomination, if they do allow women as pastors, limit females to being the pastors of women, teens, or children. The boundary line is firmly set when it comes to teaching or pastoring adult men. Years earlier, when my husband suggested it was time to move out of our busy city, I reminded him that I wouldn't likely be able to get a church job I'd enjoy in a small town, as there are more opportunities for women in the urban centres. I was being pragmatic, not cynical (well, maybe a little cynical) when I told my twenty-five-year-old male intern that he had better career opportunities than I did.

I never attended another Sunday service at my church. The elders read my resignation letter to the congregation, and there was genuine shock from the people. Stories from that day filtered back to me. The smugness of The Owners who had "won." Two women high-fiving each other in the lobby. Two women! But mostly, I received non-stop emails and phone calls from the people who cared for me. In the upheaval and heartbreak of those weeks, I briefly read all the messages and tucked them away in a file. They would sit there for a few years before I read them again—as I wrote this book.

It's a common misconception that pastors only work on Sundays; it's a trope we often joke about. But it's not true. I might not have been attending Sunday services anymore, but I had plenty to do to get things ready for the transitional pastor and to prepare the staff for the changeover. Even with the emotional turmoil of my resignation, I still felt the responsibility that everything should run smoothly, so there was no "checking out" as I prepared everything for my successor.

On my final day of work at the end of November, I went alone into the sanctuary and sat on the stairs that led up to the stage. I didn't turn any lights on, but the afternoon sun shone through the large orange-and-yellow tinted windows, creating a feeling of dusk in the room. It was time to say goodbye. In the large room of monochromatic beiges and browns, the red neon sign over the doors at the back of the room yelled out "EXIT." I pulled out my phone and took a picture of it—concrete evidence of that moment.

It was hard to believe. I had been led through many open doors to this moment. For over fifteen years, I moved from one church leadership position to the next, my confidence and skill set growing with every transition. When I decided to go to seminary, the application process went smoothly. The associate pastor of my church left at the exact time I graduated, allowing me to apply for his position. I transitioned easily from associate pastor to interim lead pastor. But now, I was being shown another door, one I had never anticipated. I had no choice but to depart through it. My heart was filled with emptiness as I left the church that day.

The next day was December. I didn't have the mental energy to figure out what I was supposed to do at that moment, so I decided to take the month off and enjoy the Christmas holidays. Next steps were for the new year.

Instead, I decided I needed to go to Rivendell. Not the magical land of hobbits, elves, and wizards, but the Rivendell Retreat Centre on Bowen Island, just a twenty-minute ferry ride from Vancouver. I needed some time to myself, so I booked four days there. Their website advertised little one-room cabins in the woods for the person craving some alone time. A wood stove would provide the heat. I could do that; I'm capable of making a fire. There was no toilet but a pot that could be emptied at the main building in the morning. Instantly, I realized I didn't need to be that alone. The lodge would be just fine.

My room (with its full bathroom) provided the ambiance of a cabin in the woods with its rustic furniture and views of the surrounding forest. The centre was high on a hill with incredible views of Howe Sound and its beautiful waters. Life was calm there, and each guest was encouraged to embrace silence and solitude. Visitors didn't speak to each other unless it was brief and consensual. Crossing paths in the hallway did not demand eye contact nor a greeting of any kind. There was space in the large kitchen for me to prepare my own meals. Many people fasted; perhaps they were the ones who used the forest cabins.

I had been there once before. I had belonged to a pastors' group, each leader from a different church in the city, who met monthly to connect and encourage each other. We had come to Rivendell for a few days during the previous year. I had been the only female in the group, but the men made every effort to make me feel comfortable. We hiked the trails on the island and ate our meals together, but mostly spent time on our own, finding renewal from our busy lives on the mainland.

One afternoon, we dropped in at one of the local coffee shops for a snack and began engaging in casual conversation, as people do when spending a few days together. When pastors get together, they talk "shop" just like any other profession. I'm not sure why we were discussing the subject of women in leadership, but one young pastor expressed his determined opinion that he didn't agree that women should be pastors. Sigh. I liked him and he was only expressing his viewpoint. The older pastors diplomatically shared their differing thoughts on the subject without trying to make him feel diminished. I sat there, thinking how odd it was that it was acceptable to express why I didn't belong while he sat right across the table from me.

My guess is that he felt he was approaching the topic matter-of-factly. I knew his comments weren't an expression of dislike toward me. From his vantage point, he was just sharing his opinion. We can agree to disagree, can't we? But it stung because what I heard was *I like you but what you're doing is wrong*. What he didn't realize was that his theology could not be separated from the woman sitting in front of him. It was just one small blip on a beautiful retreat.

Now I had returned for my second visit to Rivendell and was already familiar with the rhythms of the place. It wasn't mandatory, but every day at 8 a.m. and 5 p.m., all visitors were invited to come to the chapel in the woods. It was a single circular room with windows filling the walls, letting the outside in. As guests entered, they would find a chair or cushion on the floor along the wall. Everyone sat in a circle, allowing them to face the small table in the middle of the room. There burned a candle—its flicker reminding each of us of the presence of God, who is always with us. After the host shared a short Scripture, poem, or words from a song, we'd sit quietly for thirty minutes. Sitting in silence is helped by the natural peer pressure of the others in the room. I found that the first few minutes of stillness were the most difficult, as I wrestled with the uncomfortableness of being alone with my thoughts. But having others in the room ensured that I didn't get up and go for a walk instead.

On my first evening there, the host surprised me by asking the group to introduce ourselves to each other. Her instructions were for us to share our names, why we came on retreat, and where we put our hope. I was immediately to her left, which meant I was going first. I knew to keep it brief, as talking was not the purpose of being here.

"My name's Michelle. My job as a pastor just ended, so I'm here to reflect on what is next in my life. I put my hope in Jesus."

Next person. Lovely lady with long locks, loose clothes, and a soft voice. "It's my birthday on Thursday, and that's also the date of the new moon. I'm here to connect with the Divine. I put my hope in the moon."

Next person. "I'm taking a sabbatical from my job." And around the circle we went, most people sharing things from the Christian world in which I was familiar.

Finally, we came to the last young man. "My name is James, and I'm here because I don't know where to put my hope."

My heart broke for him. He kept his head down while speaking, neither smiling nor looking anyone in the eye. His words were draped with desperation. The pastor and mother in me wanted to talk to him, to offer solace and a listening ear. But that was not for me to do.

After our time of silence, I was alone with the retreat host and commented that everyone was certainly on different journeys. Her words continue to linger with me: "We are unapologetically Christian, but we are a safe place for everyone to discover God."

In the quiet of the following days, I began to journal. This was not a typical practice for me because I've always said, "People read your crap when you die." But being alone with your thoughts is a powerful exercise, and I wanted to ensure I had a record of what was happening in my interior life. I kept thinking of the young man who didn't know where to put his hope. I started to imagine having a church in our home, where everyone would feel welcome. It didn't matter who you were or what you believed, but we could gather over a meal and have conversations about faith and life. We could provide a safe place for anyone to discover God at their own pace. So many ideas were swirling around in my head, and I wanted to document them all.

On my final morning at Rivendell, I attended the silent chapel time once more before catching the ferry back to Vancouver. The thirty minutes of silence were done, and the others had slipped their shoes on at the door and quietly left the building. I sat alone for a while, staring at the lit candle in the centre of the room. Suddenly, I "saw" a train in front of me. It was going full steam over the tops of mountains, and it was filled with people. The train was so full that people were hanging out the windows because everyone was squeezed in so tightly. Instinctively, I knew that this train represented the church, not just the people who gather in one building on a Sunday morning, but collectively all the people in the world who love God. It was a good thing.

Then I saw some more people. They were on a distant mountaintop way over to the right, and *they wanted to get on that train!* But they couldn't. The train was not going in that direction to pick them up, and they couldn't come to the train because of the deep valley in between the mountains. For about one minute, I was left with this predicament: "God, these people want to get on the train. How are they going to get on it?" I had such angst for them. It wasn't fair. They desperately wanted to be on the train but had no access to it.

Then it happened. I saw a smaller train come off the first and veer right toward the people on the far mountaintop. It wasn't an audible voice, but I distinctly heard God say to me, "*You be the train who goes and gets those people.*"

CHAPTER 21

Loveables

When I returned home from Rivendell, I shared with John my vision of the train and the plans for a house church where everyone would be welcome. He was as enthusiastic as I was. We had so many friends who no longer went to church but still wanted to be in a faith community. Other friends had partners who had no interest in attending a traditional church. But church on a Monday night. With dinner. In somebody's house. Sign me up!

It must have been providence, but a month later, I met a man named Andy. He had already been doing this type of house church for many years. He and his friends met in different homes throughout the Vancouver area, and then once a month, they would all gather for a shared meal and service. They called it Simple Church.[16] Most of the superfluous stuff of religious organizations gone. Just friends. A meal. Faith conversations. Prayer. Simple.

Meeting Andy was incredibly opportune, as he was able to share his wisdom and experience with me. Some of the Simple Churches invited us to visit so we could observe how each group functioned. It was March 2020, and we were excited to start church in our home. But it was March 2020! Only a few weeks later, we realized the pandemic was going to change things. Our

16 Simplechurches.ca

first modification was to move our communal meals to the back yard, as small gatherings were still allowed in our province if they were outside. By autumn, our group ceased eating together, as sharing food posed too many risks, and finally, in November of that year, we had to stop altogether. COVID-19 was dictating the social norms, and we were not permitted to gather. It was no longer just John and I who were about to experience what it felt like to lose an in-person faith community.

It was also in March 2020 when I thought it would be a good time to return to the job market. Wrong! Little did I know as I started to submit résumés in the non-profit sector that everything was about to shut down due to a world pandemic. I guess I would be on a break for a bit longer.

How would I pass my days with no job and limited social interactions due to pandemic restrictions? I needed a new paradigm on how to see myself. Who was I now? What was I going to do for work? I just spent fifteen years working toward a goal, and now it was completely gone. And COVID and its consequences had stripped me of the ability to move forward.

If I couldn't go out and work, then I needed to do something that felt purposeful. I remembered something the Rivendell retreat host did, which sparked an idea in me. At one of the chapel times, she instructed us to take a glass bead and place it on the table with the candle. It was to represent a person or a situation that felt impossible, but we were going to release that concern to God; there are some things only he can do. Each of the people in the room took a bead and placed it in front of the candle. I was greedy; I took six. I started with one bead but then kept thinking of more people who were in difficult situations, so my bead count increased. During the four days I was there, no one removed them from the table, and those beads sat in front of the candle every day, reminding me that I had turned my concerns for these people over to the care of God.

Prompted by this memory, I went to Michael's craft store and bought a container and some clear glass beads. I made my own prayer jar and decided that if I couldn't get a job, then this would be it. I wrote the name of a friend or family member who was special to me on forty different beads. I rarely did the "laundry list" prayers. You know the type: "Here, God, here's a list of all the things I'd like for this person." Rather, one by one, I would put the beads in my palm and imagine placing them before God. Each day, I'd ask for something different, often as simple as wanting them to know how much God loves them. It was time consuming, but when you don't have a job, or children at home, or you're not even allowed to meet with others, all of a sudden, there's time.

Not long afterwards, I was out for a walk, chatting with a friend on the phone. She had some exciting news to share with me. "A friend of ours is like a different person. It all started on December 8." She continued to excitedly share all the positive changes in this person's life; she spoke of the end of destructive habits and the restoration of some relationships. But all I could hear was "December 8." I had to calm myself down and listen to her properly because I was so excited to hear her say that date. When she finished speaking, I could hardly wait to pose the question: "Do you know what happened on December 8?" I shared my story with her. Our mutual friend was the first bead—the first of the six beads I placed in front of the candle at Rivendell. The first person I turned all my concerns about over to God. On December 8.

My prayer beads also contributed to something I hadn't expected. One evening, I was reading a famous sermon that Jesus gave, and his words gripped me. Here's a paraphrase: Everybody says that you should love your friends and hate your enemies, but I'm challenging that. I'm telling you to love your enemies. Show them kindness when they give you a hard time. This is what God does. Anyone can give love to the loveable. Even an evil person can do that. Are you no better than that?[17]

Even an evil person can love the loveable. Am I no better than that?

I instantly knew what I needed to do. The next morning, I was going to prepare a second prayer jar and put the names of all the people who had hurt me in it. I went to sleep peacefully, but in the morning, I felt the gentle but overwhelming nudge to do more. Jesus said to treat your enemies like the people you love. I knew my instructions: put the names of the people who hurt me in the same jar with the people whom I love and mix them up together. Treat everyone like a loveable.

It seemed I now had another assignment from Dr. Love—not my seminary professor but the origin of Divine Love himself. This was a huge step in my forgiveness process. And it was a process. Forgiveness takes time. I would continue to hear stories or untruths that were hurtful, and sometimes I would pick up the prayer bead with the offender's name on it and go "Pffft!" There was no love in my heart for them. It was on those days that I had to pray for my own heart rather than theirs.

Every day, I prayed over the pile of glass beads in my lap. As the months ticked by, I started to realize that they were replacing the pile of pebbles that was my woundedness. I was undoing that imaginary pile as I picked up one bead at a time, offered it to God, and then returned it to the glass container.

This new pile of pebbles was for my healing.

With all my free time, I was able to engage in another immensely helpful process. I participated in the Ignatius Spiritual Exercises: nine months of prayer exercises. The restrictions of the pandemic were difficult, but one of its gifts was the

....

17   Matthew 5:43–47 (The Message). This is my paraphrase from The Message version of the Bible.

ability to do things I would not normally have time for.

Ignatius of Loyola was a privileged young man who lived in the sixteenth century. His life was centred around superficial pursuits, which ended when he injured his leg during his military service. As he recuperated at home, he asked that his favourite genre of novel be brought to him to pass the time. But instead of the romance novels he requested, he was brought literary works of Jesus Christ. It completely changed the direction of his life.

He developed a series of prayer exercises, which are still being used five hundred years later. He intended that participants would use them on a spiritual retreat—five hours a day for thirty days. But even back then, most people did not have a month to commit to such a practice, so it was adapted to five hours a week for thirty weeks. Good thing, because even during the pandemic, I didn't have that much spare time.

Each day, I would read the assigned Bible verses, poem, or prayer activity, and then I would sit with God for an hour. No speaking on my part; my task was to listen. After listening to what God would impress on my heart for that hour, I would journal about it for about fifteen minutes. (Recognizing how difficult it is to sit for a whole hour and just listen, five extra weeks are added at the beginning of the program because most people, including myself, are unaccustomed to sitting still for a whole hour.)

Every month, I would meet with my spiritual director, the woman who was my companion on this spiritual journey. A second monthly meeting included two male pastors who were also doing the Ignatian exercises. Pandemic restrictions were still in place, but fortunately, Zoom enabled us to meet regularly. At our final session, we were asked to share what we noticed about each other's spiritual journeys. I had put much effort into reflecting on what they had shared over the previous nine months so that I had encouragements to share with them both. But when it was their turn to share their observations about me,

I was disappointed. They didn't have much to say other than to express amazement that I wasn't bitter after everything I had been through. One of the men said, "You seem happy, buoyant even." *That's it? I'm not bitter but happy. That's all you have to offer?*

I already knew that. I was disappointed because I had hoped for new insights about my spiritual journey. They could only marvel at something that was so obvious to me. I had already moved past my pain, and in their opinion, that trumped any other accomplishment.

A book had helped me with this process. It was an allegorical tale whose title is gone from my memory. But one scene remains with me. A man was in prison, and the bars were made of his bitterness. The people who had wronged him were going on about their lives, not even realizing this man was still locked up. And even if they did, they could not release him because the bars were of his own making. It is only I who can set myself free from the bars of bitterness. And so that's what I did—I broke myself out.

It was around this time that I had a revelation. I noticed that throughout all the opposition and disheartening events of the previous year, I had kept my joy. None of the low-level depression I had for the three years following my first resignation crept back at all. As awful as everything had been, and as uncertain as my life's plans felt, I experienced no sadness. I was looking forward to the future and wondering what could possibly be ahead.

I discovered that life isn't about finding joy in doing exactly what you want to do. It's about finding joy in whatever life hands you. I couldn't control the actions or attitudes of other people. But sitting quietly with God for many months taught me I didn't need to.

I did the exercises five days a week, every week, from September to May. A lot had changed within me during that time.

Nine months—isn't that typically the time it takes for new life to develop?

CHAPTER 22
Words Wound and Words Heal

He found me on Facebook. I'd never met this man, but he was a friend of a woman in the church, and she had told him my story.

"Dear Pastor Michelle,

You don't know me, and we've never met, but I've heard from a distance a tiny bit of the ordeal you've recently undergone in your congregation. For a variety of reasons, my heart broke to hear that you had resigned, that some $&%# view of doctrine was once again more important than truth or people.

For whatever it's worth, I'm so sorry, for the loss, for the frustration, for all that is unjust in being a woman in ministry.

I won't offer any platitudes or false hope that things will get better, just that I'm so sorry that this happened. It wasn't right and will never be right. But I pray that you find comfort and renewed vision for the future, that you are strengthened in your call.

Regards, _____ "

I can only imagine the "variety of reasons his heart broke" when the author of this note heard my story, but it had such a positive impact on me. As a man, he felt the injustice of being a woman and it pained him enough to reach out and communicate with me. He had no influence at my church nor power to change anything, but he gave me a glimpse of his empathy and that was enough. How often do we (me included) hear a story, feel saddened by it for a bit, but then move on? "What can we do?" we ask ourselves. This man took a few moments to send a note of encouragement through Facebook Messenger to someone he didn't even know.

It didn't fix my situation, but it helped to fix me.

Immediately after my resignation, the e-mails came rolling in. Here is a small sampling:

From a man:

> *"Our church has suffered a massive loss with your leaving. Not only were you and John long-serving members of the body, but your vision, passion, and leadership were sorely needed. This is not fair. I feel pretty appalled at the injustice. If people who disagreed had nonetheless acted with love and respect for their brothers and sisters, we wouldn't be here right now. We would have been able to have a vote and hear the voice of the church and move on."*

From a woman:

> *"I am gutted to hear that you and John have had to leave the church because of how you have been treated by some of our people. I fully support your stance [of no longer showing up on Sunday mornings] because you are giving a very clear and necessary message that some need to hear. As I sat and listened to the letters being read that morning (delivered by a man, probably because no woman could stomach to read what is actually going on), I was horrified. I can't even understand how this is even a debate. I felt like I wanted to jump up and say STOP! This is wrong!! I thought of Mary, the human vessel through which Jesus was born and nursed. Where would we be without her? I felt nauseous. I know it is time to pray hard and dig deep, but I really struggle with the fact that they are taking MORE time to debate this issue. Maybe it's time for every woman to just not show up—my patience with this issue and the church is running out."*

From a couple:

> *"We really value your leadership and perspective in your teachings, and your boldness to encourage the congregation to renew the difficult conversations around their faith in a biblical and collegial manner. We think that in the midst of those hard conversations is where God would want us to live our lives so that we are actively working to love our neighbours, even with those whom we disagree."*

The last few words of this one made me chuckle:

"I was devastated when it was announced you are leaving! I needed a good cry after the service. You are an amazing pastor and friend. It's unfortunate it had to come to this point. We sure are dumb sheep sometimes."

And, finally, a sentiment to wrap them all up:

"Haters gonna hate, but don't let that stop you."

So many people delivered words of love and support. In the aftermath of my resignation, it was the angry letters that I found the most helpful. Perhaps because they paralleled my feelings at the time, but mostly because I felt those people understood. They could feel my pain. They were angry not only on my behalf but on behalf of anyone who is discriminated against because they don't fit into some falsely designed norm for a specific role.

As the weeks rolled by, the emails kept coming, many beginning with, "I meant to send this earlier…" It's hard to write those notes, to find the correct words. But do it. Your words are healing.

I still wonder why some people I considered friends and who never caused me any grief said nothing when we left the church. Why didn't they reach out with a simple goodbye? Not one word to me and my husband after all these years we had known each other. The toxic voice in my head told me it was because even though they never publicly said it, they didn't really like me. Or maybe they believed a woman shouldn't lead a church and thought it was best I leave anyway. *With her gone, things can go back to the way it used to be.* But the more reasonable voice in my head told me that they probably just didn't know what to say.

Many years ago, I heard a psychologist on a podcast say that our psyches weren't meant to carry the burdens of the entire globe, only those in our village. It can be too overwhelming to witness and process all the injustices in our world, so we change the channel or push that story to the back of our minds—actions that are often necessary to protect our mental health. We can't help everyone, but we can certainly reach out to those who are right in front of us. There is such a small cost to take the initiative to acknowledge someone's pain and offer kind words. People need to hear from us when they go through tough things—divorce, miscarriage, sickness, job loss—because if we say nothing, they will create their own narrative. *That person doesn't care about my pain.*

Jen was part of my village. She lived a couple blocks from me, and we would regularly walk our dogs together. She was also one of the elders in the church, which made her easy to talk to because she already knew the details of what was happening to me. I didn't need to be concerned that I was breaking confidences or exposing her to things she wasn't supposed to know.

One evening during the height of the drama prior to my resignation, I started venting to her and she appeared to be overwhelmed. She looked at me with true compassion. "I'm so sorry you have to go through all this and that people are treating you so terribly. I wish none of this ever happened." Those were the gist of her words. Her few short sentences held all my pain. There were no tears in her eyes or any other overly dramatic notions as we walked in silence afterwards. She understood my pain but didn't keep it inside. She said it out loud. I don't think I ever told her how much I appreciated that.

On that evening, Jen confirmed something to me that I knew already knew but realized that I needed to practise more. My words have the power to mend others, to alleviate pain. I knew of their power to hurt and endeavoured to avoid using them that way. But now I recognized that I needed to be much more intentional about using my words to help people—like the man who didn't know me but sent me a message through Facebook.

Two months after my resignation, a transitional pastor came. He was a pragmatic, direct man who had experience mediating these types of conflicts in churches, even dealing with this exact situation in his last church. He was tall, commanding, and not afraid of conflict, but also presented with a gentle authority that hopefully most would respect.

I met him at a lunch organized by a third party, and he invited me to share my side of the story. He listened carefully and intently, and when I was finished, he answered a question I hadn't even asked during our time together. "There's no way you could have stayed. Your presence needs to be gone for the church to figure out this mess." It meant so much to have someone in authority finally affirm my decision. Up until then, well-meaning people kept encouraging me to stay, to work with the church through this difficult time, but all I heard was *Stay, continue to be in this toxic environment with no one to support you.* I was able to exhale. My decision to leave was finally supported by someone who had experience in these matters, and his words released me from any lingering guilt that perhaps I was letting my church down.

The baton was now being passed to him, and I was able to stop running. When I started as interim lead pastor, I knew I was going to be used for change, one way or the other. Either I was going to be the first female lead pastor in the denomination (other than a brief stint by a woman in the 1940s) or my departure would spur some change. The former wasn't going to happen, so let's see about the latter.

CHAPTER 23
I Know How You Feel

I had never been suspected of shoplifting before. When I entered the drugstore, I noticed the young security guard as I whisked through the doors and headed toward the cosmetics aisle. As I scoured the display, looking for a specific item, the familiar sound of my phone receiving a text alerted my ear. With Pavlovian swiftness, I opened my purse, assessed that the message required no immediate answer, and returned my phone to my bag.

Within seconds, the security guard was standing so close to me that if I bent my elbow, it would have touched him. I knew instinctively why he was there and didn't blame him for it, but I also knew I had done nothing wrong. To ease the awkwardness of the situation, I addressed him with a hello and asked him how his day was going. I then proceeded to take my sweet time finding what I was looking for. I had no fear because I knew that even if he asked to look in my purse, he would find nothing.

It wasn't until I had paid for my product and was out in my car that I realized the immensity of my White privilege that day. In my over fifty years on this earth, no one has ever accused me of stealing. Not for a moment did I worry that I would end up in trouble. I had lived my entire life knowing that I would be believed, or that even if they looked in my purse, I would be released with the apologies afforded me even though I had given the security guard good reason for his suspicions.

And that's when it hit me. The Black Lives Matter slogan had been around for a few years, and books on White privilege had hit the bookstores. Even though I thought I understood what those things meant, this was the first time I had an experience that showed me how my White privilege affected my way in the world. I knew the stories and complaints that people of colour had shared about being followed in stores simply because of the colour of their skin, to be suspected of something of which they were completely innocent, but until it happened to me, I couldn't fully empathize with the experience of people of colour.

I needed that lesson. It helped me understand why others failed to appreciate everything I was experiencing. I can hear people's stories, sympathize, and offer support the best I can, and sometimes that can be sufficient to understand their plight. But it's when I have experiences that help me understand what it's like for people who are different than me that I start to have those "a-ha" moments. It's then I start to encounter empathy.

Research professor and author Brené Brown explains how this response creates a connection between people.[18] Sympathy takes some effort with kind words, a prepared meal, or perhaps a donation toward a good cause, but it doesn't require an emotional connection. To feel empathy for someone, on the other hand, means that you will hurt, at least a little, on the other's behalf. Empathy requires that you connect to something within yourself that connects to the emotions of the other person.

My friend shared that until her own mother died, she simply didn't understand the pain of losing a parent. When others

....

18 Brené Brown, Katy Davis, Al Francis-Sears, and Abi Stephenson, "Brené Brown on Empathy vs. Sympathy," filmed April 1, 2016 via RSA, London, UK, animated short, 2:53, https://www.youtube.com/watch?v=KZBTY ViDP1Q.

lost loved ones, she offered condolences, signed the card, and donated toward the flowers, but now she understands the pain. It wasn't until she had experienced the same loss herself that she was truly able to empathize.

An elderly pastor friend from my church lost his wife after sixty years of marriage. Throughout his many years in the pastorate, he had given care to many grieving spouses. Now that it was his turn to receive care from others, he noticed, however, that he received the greatest solace and wisdom from those who had been widowed before him because he knew they understood his pain.

When a friend of mine decided that she needed to deal with her alcohol consumption, I attended a few Alcoholics Anonymous meetings with her. I watched as participants were transparent about their addiction and shared honestly about their failings of the previous week. None of their stories were met with judgement or any shame-inducing words but a simple clap and a thank you. Everyone in the room treated the others with respect and dignity because they could completely empathize with their journey. The people who had been sober for years didn't boast a superiority over those who had only been dry a few days because they understood the struggle and how one mistake could lead them to the same place. I leaned over to my friend and said, "This is what church should be like."

Empathy is emotional unity. *I see you, I hear you, I understand your pain, and I care.*

What would it take for men to truly understand what women go through? The Huichol tribe in Mexico believes that when a woman is going through the pains of childbirth, the husband should feel the pain as well. A string is tied to her husband's testicles, and she pulls on it each time she experiences a painful contraction.[19] What

19   Nicholas D. Kristof and Sheryl WuDunn, *Half the Sky: Turning Oppression into Opportunity for Women Worldwide* (New York, NY: Knopf Press, 2009), location 2252, Kindle.

a beautiful story of desiring to understand the other's pain. But even I think that might be a bit overkill!

Within weeks of my resignation, the board wrote a letter apologizing to me and the church. Before the elders read it to the congregation, the letter was sent to me for my feedback. As I read it, I was concerned that the wording watered down the truth of my experience. The letter stated that I was quitting due to uncomfortable circumstances and harsh words directed my way. Really? Is that all that happened to me? I appreciated that they allowed me to give input but told them that this statement was not strong enough.

I reminded them that I was leaving because of the continual slander directed at me that wasn't being shut down. I was accused of being demonic, leading the church into apostasy, and being a false teacher. Emails were circulating not only about the proposed bylaw change but complaining about me. Two of my staff members' jobs were threatened because they supported me. Some people turned their backs to me and walked away when I greeted them on Sunday mornings. My husband, who is congenial and gets along with everybody, refused to walk through the church doors anymore because he no longer felt welcome. To say that I was leaving because of "harsh words" implied a few people said some hurtful things and I couldn't handle it. After years of being a woman in church leadership, I had developed a thick skin. I was not leaving because a few people said some nasty things.

The letter was revised.

The final draft, which was emailed to all the church members, apologized to John and me, stating that the elders hadn't addressed this matter in a timely fashion. The letter spoke of the continuing false and damaging statements meant to harm my reputation, which forced me to reluctantly step down from my position. I appreciated their words. They were a gift to my reputation. But I had wished for more.

Words couldn't really encapsulate my experience of marginalization during my time as interim pastor or my many years in church leadership—because how can others truly understand something when all they see is the small pebbles? A story that makes them groan. Hearing someone say untruths about me. Reading a difficult email from a congregant. Feeling sad when I share an experience of exclusion.

I was never physically attacked or hurt. I wasn't fired from my job. I seemed to be thriving. All people see are the individual pebbles. That's not such a big deal, they think. But they don't see the large pile of pebbles, the constant addition of stones, all accumulated into one big mound. I could sense their weight even when I wasn't under them. And finally… one small stone is added, and the weight becomes too much.

After my resignation, the empathy I received from other people helped: the elder who cried out in pain over what happened to me; the friends in the church who were so angry on my behalf—an anger caused by frustration at a system of discrimination. When people got angry on my behalf, it felt so supportive because I couldn't carry all the anger by myself; sometimes I needed to go to sorrow and let others carry the anger for me.

I believe that this support is the reason I did not experience any depression when I left the church, just resignation with my resignation. When I quit my job the first time, no one acknowledged how much I loved it and how hard it was for me to leave. *You've decided to leave? OK.* Every week that passed was so painful because I was alone in my pain. My second resignation was different. It was more difficult, but I received support.

There was one person whose empathy helped me out more than any other. It's so tempting to think of God as far away or disinterested in our human lives, but because he had experienced being human, I believe he was able to fully empathize with my journey (well, almost fully, because he wasn't a woman).

Most of the people who lashed out at Jesus weren't the average person on the street but the religious leaders and the church insiders. That sounded familiar.

They called him a demon. I've heard that one!

They accused him of speaking untruths. Check!

He had a friend who went behind his back and betrayed him. I know how that feels.

In the face of the power structures of those who opposed Jesus, many of his friends didn't stand up for him. I understood that loneliness.

But…

He continued to love and encourage the friends who ran away when things got tough.

He let his betrayer sit at his table, and he washed his feet.

He never stopped speaking his truths even when people attacked and accused him.

Jesus forgave the people who hurt him. And they hadn't even asked for forgiveness.

That's real power. That's love.

I had read these stories many times before, but in the year after my resignation, this time, I connected with them differently. Now life felt a little less lonely. God knew exactly how I felt because he had been through it too.

CHAPTER 24
Courage

Fear Factor. When my kids were younger that was our favourite television show. We relished the adrenaline rush while we watched others attempt tasks that we'd never dream of doing: enduring bee stings, doing high-altitude stunts, eating bugs. In 2006, we took a family vacation to California and were excited that Universal Studios had its own *Fear Factor* stage show. It wasn't the TV show but a modified event suitable for guests at the park. As we lined up to enter the theatre, a young man who worked at the studio approached me and asked if I'd like to participate in the next show. My seven- and ten-year-olds looked at me with pure glee. "You must!"

My stomach started to feel a little queasy, and I asked him what my participation would entail.

The man explained that he had to ask me a couple of questions first.

"Are you pregnant?"

"No."

"Are you allergic to bee stings?"

"No, but I don't want to be stung."

He assured me that I (probably) wouldn't get stung. "Remember this is Universal Studios, not the TV show. You're not going to get hurt. But before I tell you the challenge, you must agree to do it."

I gave him a tentative yes and he explained, "We are going to put your head in a plexiglass box. You'll have earplugs, goggles, and a mask to cover the orifices in your head. We will bring your husband up on the stage, and he will spin a big wheel. Whatever the dial lands on, we will put five of that creature in the box with you. Five snakes, five spiders, five scorpions, or five cockroaches."

I immediately felt ill. My children begged me to do it. In the stress of making the final decision, I said to my husband, "I don't need to do this. I don't need to prove myself to anyone." But my children's pleas won out and I agreed.

To help calm my nerves, the worker told me that he had selected me because I had thick hair. He said, "Don't worry, we do this with the animals every day. They are bored with it. We will put them on the top of your head, and they will likely just sit there. Just don't move your head."

Our children were sitting in the front row with my camera, as cell phones weren't commonplace then. My husband was sitting beside them, waiting to be invited onto the stage. My head was in a box. John came up and spun the big *Wheel of Fortune*-type wheel. I couldn't see him because he was off to the side, but I could hear the squeals of anticipation from the audience. It occurred to me at that moment that I needed to listen to find out what was going in the box with me. Would I be able to hear with the earplugs?

Scorpions. I didn't even have time to decide if I was all right with that. Before I was able to process whether that was the least of all evils I could encounter, the top pane of the plexiglass box was opened and I could feel the first of the large black arachnids placed on my head. (Yes, they are part of the spider family!) It immediately crawled over my left eye, which fortunately was protected by the goggles. He was soon joined by four of his friends, each of them measuring about seven inches long. I was told that I only had to endure it for a minute, but I'm quite certain it was much longer, as the host of the event was enjoy-ing engaging with the audience. I went to my happy place. In my mind, I was at a beach, watching the imaginary waves roll in. I slowly wiggled my fingers and toes to calm my thumping heart. I had no choice but to obey my pre-show instructions. No sudden moves. My only job was to stay still.

Then the lights in the building went out and the crowd cooed, "Oooooh!" They were Madagascar scorpions, which luminesced green in the dark. So now my head was in a box with five scorpi-ons in complete darkness. Somehow, they forgot to tell me that detail. Stay still. It will be over soon. And it was. One by one the animals were removed from the top of my head, and I was released from the box. As I got up from my chair, I looked over to the other side of the stage, and there were four large aquariums full of creatures. Tarantulas crawling all over each other, snakes ensnarled together—I'm sure it was just for effect to provide the ick factor for the audience, but if I had seen that before my head went in the box, I wouldn't have done it.

I have two distinct positive memories from that day. The first was the incredible sense of accomplishment of doing something that terrified me. The second was that my ten-year-old son told me I was his hero.

Courage is an interesting thing, not always inherent. That day, I was a hero to a ten- and seven-year-old, but not because I was intrinsically brave. I hate spiders, but if necessary, I'd sit in a tub of them to protect my children. Courage isn't always an inner quality we already have; it often arises when our love of something or someone is greater than our fear of what is hurting the thing we love.

When we are motivated by the right things, we become very courageous.

For years, I had to find the boldness to work within a system of patriarchy and misogyny, and I managed because I was motivated by something greater: I wanted to change things for the next generation of women. And in my more hopeful moments, I also wanted to improve things for myself and other women presently in leadership positions. So when I was treated condescendingly, I responded graciously. When I was ignored by the men in the room, I showed interest in them and started conversations about subjects of their liking. For years, I stayed within the system so I could help facilitate change. When I finally decided to quit my job, it wasn't a knee-jerk reaction or a fearful run-for-your-life determination. I knew that the point had finally come when my departure would be more helpful to the cause than my remaining. It was time for me to leave so that my church community could rally together and make positive change. Leaving wasn't an act of cowardice; it took bravery to leave the security of a great job, the community of a church family, and the dreams I had regarding my role in my church.

I believe everyone wants to be treated equally, but in this unjust world, that doesn't just happen on its own. Words possess an incredible amount of power; they can change the trajectory of someone's life. They can inspire movements and rally people. But we often don't arrive at equality until we move beyond words and take action. Encouraging words are not enough to someone buried under the weight of oppression; we must fight for their rights as well. The heart of the people must become the law of the people—justice! And that takes courage. Because when you fight for the rights of others, it often comes with a cost to yourself.

In the movie *The Butler*, there's a scene where the son, Louis, is with his friends, participating at a sit-in at a restaurant. They are occupying seats at the service counter that were reserved for White people. The White patrons of the restaurant screamed and spat at the protesters. Among the protesters sat one White man who was mistreated along with his Black friends, but he is not the one to be applauded. It is the people of colour who endured, persisted, and fought for their freedom who are the heroes. But change is accelerated when empathy prompts the people who possess power and privilege to join the fight for equality. The one White man was willing to endure the abuse that the Black people dealt with all the time, with the hope of inducing change.

Men are joining in the fight for women's equality, and sometimes quite literally. In December 2021, Members of Parliament in Jordan had a fistfight right in the legislature over the rights of women in their country.[20] Jordanian women have equal rights concerning health care, education, employment, and participation in politics, but do not have the same rights with their nationality or citizenship. For example, they can't pass their nationality on to their children or spouses. These fisticuffs in parliament were prompted by proposed changes to their constitution. Hmmm. Sounds familiar.

Fistfights are not what is needed, but the anger that provokes them can fuel the action that is necessary for change—a healthy anger that propels men and women to demand that women be treated equally. It takes courage to challenge the status quo, to risk losing or damaging your own reputation or position to stand up for others who do not have the same privileges. Verbal support is not enough; equality is a result of action.

A year after leaving my job, November 2020, all the drama of the previous year felt like a distant memory, seen only in the rearview mirror. Most of the time, I was able to push the events from my mind.

My husband and I were spending a Sunday afternoon strolling in the picturesque waterfront town of Steveston, a suburb of Vancouver. The name "Storybook" covered many of its main

20   Celine Alkhaldi, "Jordan MPs Trade Blows Amid Heated Discussion on Women's Rights," CTV News, accessed April 10, 2022, https://www.ctvnews.ca/world/jordan-mps-trade-blows-amid-heated-discussion-on-women-s-rights-1.5722857.

street buildings, as it's where the American TV show *Once Upon a Time* was filmed. It was a beautiful fall day, and I waited on the boardwalk as John headed down onto the pier to buy some salmon for dinner. As I waited for him, two young women asked me to take their photo. I did so, even though I didn't want to touch their phone because I might get COVID. Remember those days? But they were so nice, I took the risk. When John returned, we continued down the promenade, feeling relaxed in the sun and the crisp breeze.

My phone started to ping. *Ping. Ping. Ping.* It was coming alive. I was receiving so many texts. I didn't want to interrupt being present in the beautiful, serene setting, but I couldn't resist the urge to look. I was aware that it was the day my church was finally voting on the bylaw. I pulled out my phone without breaking my stride. I read the first text: the bylaw passed. I mentioned it to my husband. He acknowledged that he heard me, and we kept walking in silence.

I had expected to feel completely detached from the results. They no longer had anything to do with me; I was gone and would never be returning. But a contentment filled me. No euphoria or victorious excitement, but just a sense of thankfulness that all I had gone through was not wasted. Everything I had experienced moved the dimmer switch up a bit for women. In one church, in one town, there was no longer a barrier to women in leadership. One of the text messages made me smile: "Thank you, Pastor Michelle. Your sacrifice has paved the way for all the women coming up behind you."

So many losses to obtain one small gain. Equality is a slow process.

The following March, my then-adult daughter called me on International Women's Day and thanked me for everything I had done for women. I felt like a superhero once again.

CHAPTER 25
A Seat for Everyone

Simple encounters can teach the biggest lessons. Through my participation with SoulFood and our church's involvement with the Mat Program, I became involved with our city's Housing and Homelessness Task Group. This committee included municipal leaders, police, and representatives from social programs and churches. At our monthly meetings, twenty-five people sat around a large table. After those seats were filled, additional people took the seats in a second circle behind them. Those participants sat in chairs but were not seated around the table.

One month, I failed to arrive early and entered the room just as the meeting had begun. I approached the final few chairs around the table but noticed that there were three women whom I'd not met before sitting in the outer circle. It didn't seem right that I would take a seat at the table if they had arrived before me. So I turned to them and offered, "You were here first. Would you ladies like to sit here at the table?"

They indicated that they were fine where they were, but as I took my seat, I heard one woman say to the others, "She called us ladies!" I didn't understand her seemingly strange comment until later in the meeting. As our three guests gave a presentation on addiction and homelessness from their personal experiences, I started to gain clarity. It was my greeting of "ladies" that surprised them, even though I would have used that term for any woman sitting in those seats. Perhaps they were not accustomed to being addressed with respect. Or after years of living on the marginalized sidelines, did they feel they didn't deserve a place at the table? Their polite refusal to join the inner circle of the meeting that day reminded me why I was always drawn to working with people from marginalized groups. No one should feel this way.

My memories of working at the church are a blend of joy and pain. How I loved my job. The people. Helping them feel connected to others. The projects that enabled our congregants to feel part of our community. I enjoyed teaching and inspiring people to live their lives through the lens of God's love for everybody. It has always been my dream that the church should be a place where everyone would feel embraced, including those who think they might not fit in or be welcome. After I left the church, the loss was great. I realized that I might never have a position like that again. But I've learned to accept this loss. Sometimes trailblazers get burned, but if it clears the way for others following the same path, it's worth it.

A year after I left my job, I looked at John, who was sitting across from me at the dining room table, and said, "Let's move to Vancouver Island." And he instantly agreed. Little emotion accompanied the decision. We just both knew it was time for a change. He had a new job and was able to work from home. The real estate market was booming. We could be closer to my mother, who still lived in my childhood home by the ocean. Our son had moved to a surfing community on the west coast of the Island, and I had lots of extended family there. And we both looked forward to the slower pace of island living. We always knew we'd go back to the Island eventually, perhaps when we retired. But with the recent circumstances of my job combined with pandemic-prompted life changes, our moving date moved up ten to fifteen years.

We sold our home very quickly, and by the end of the year, we had found a new place to live in a quaint beach town not far from where I grew up. We had decided that we only needed a small house for the two of us, but that's not what we purchased. When we saw it, we knew it was the house for us. Over ninety Douglas fir and red cedar trees give the property a park-like feeling, and the slanted ceilings and skylights of the west coast-style home give it the air of a retreat centre. A tree fort is nestled in the back yard. Deer and bunnies are our constant visitors. Due to its "woodsy" park-like feel, our daughter dubbed our new home "the cabin," even though it's the biggest house and piece of property we've ever owned. Oh, and the beach is a few short blocks away.

We took possession of our house in the spring. John busied himself in his new job and appointed himself as general contractor over all the renovations. My contribution at the time was a little less taxing. It was the beginning of a month's long heat wave, so the dog and I sat in the back yard, trying to keep cool, staying out of the way of the trades workers, and just generally decompressing from all the events of the previous year.

We were drawn to the house for the potential it had; we quickly developed a similar vision for it. Dated pink carpets were replaced with wood flooring. While the floors were torn up, the electrical was updated and all the old Poly-B plumbing was replaced. The forty-year-old kitchen and bathrooms were redone. We didn't have enough furniture to fill the place, but Facebook marketplace helped us complete the job.

There was just one final piece of furniture we wanted that would fit with the philosophy of our new home: a round dining room table—a *large* round dining room table. We found a local woodworker who was up for the task. He made it from locally salvaged red cedar trees. Resin was poured into all the nooks and crannies of the wood, allowing us to see the floor through the knot holes. A local welder crafted a beautiful iron pedestal for it to balance on. Inspired by the train I "saw" while at Rivendell, our new dining room table was going to be a place where everyone could gather, a place where all would be welcome. There is no "head of the table" at a circular table; everyone sits with equal prominence.

Our home became a sanctuary not just for us but for friends and family who needed a place to get away. And I think they all got the memo. Any thoughts of being disconnected from our friends at the church were quickly remedied. Whether it's that people weren't ready yet for post-COVID international travel or that Vancouver Island is a frequent vacation spot for city dwellers, our guest rooms have rarely been empty, especially during the warmer months.

I continued being intentional about releasing any remaining anger or bitterness from the previous years. Occasionally, I realized that even though my wounds had greatly healed, they were still vulnerable to injury. I had to learn that even though I had moved on, others had not. A random phone call to one of our guests from someone I'd never met stung for a few days. Our guest told his caller that he was staying with us, and the person on the other end of the line asked if that was wise. He had heard things about me, from someone who doesn't even attend the church. Third-hand news. My husband and our friends had a good chuckle about how ridiculous this was, and I laughed along with them. But I could feel the bitterness well up. Two years later, people were still slandering me. It took a few days for me to cease ruminating and realize that I had no control over what other people thought of me or what versions of the truth they thought they had. My job was to forgive, and I couldn't control what anyone else did.

I chose to redirect my energies. When someone from my past would reach out and poke my wounds, I discovered that the best way to prevent my prison bars of bitterness from reconstructing was to put love into action. I had to shift my emotions into something more helpful. Instead of focusing on the recent offence, I would ask myself, "Who needs a word of encouragement today? How can I practically help someone who is feeling marginalized or sad?" It's a trade-off that always makes me feel better—intentional positive action over self-pity and bitterness. Healing of my hurts began when I refused to give others what they gave me.

It was time to move on to the next phase of my life. If I could go back to school and start a new career at forty-seven, then I could certainly do it again. In his *The Art of Happiness* podcast, Harvard professor Arthur Brooks challenges his mid-life listeners. He explains that when you are in your mid-fifties, you're only halfway through your adult life. It is not a time to give up or feel you have nothing left to contribute to the world. You're only at the halfway point. That was a perspective I needed to hear.

I decided it was time to start writing, to share my story. The irony of my story is that my primary passion has always been to make those who feel like "others" or unwelcome at the table feel included. And yet I was not welcome. So it is time to set a new table.

There's a book called *The Great Emergence: How Christianity is Changing and Why* by Dr. Phyllis Tickle. A premise she shares in the book is that approximately every five hundred years throughout the history of Christianity, the church has a big garage sale. During these key transitional points in its history, a bunch of old and useless stuff goes out to the curb and new stuff comes in. It seems to me that part of the garage sale swap that is happening now is that *patriarchy* and *misogyny* are going in the trash and *equality* and *inclusion* are being brought in—definitely a worthy trade.

In our new town, there's a building that captured my husband's imagination when we first came to look for a house: the theatre on the main street. "I'm going to act in plays here," John said, re-envisioning his dream of acting that had been put on the back burner after we had children.

It was with great excitement that I went to watch him act in Canadian playwright Daniel MacIvor's show *How It Works*. As the lights went down and the curtains opened, one of his fellow actors opened the play with a monologue.

It took my breath away. I knew instantly that I would end my story with her words:

> As far as I can figure, the way that it works is this: everyone has something that happened to them. The thing that we each carry. And you can see it in people, if you look. See it in the way someone walks, in the way someone takes a compliment, sometimes you can just see it in someone's eyes, in one moment, of desperation, of fear, in one quick moment you can see that thing that happened. Everyone has it. The thing that keeps you up at night or makes you not trust people, or stops love. The thing that hurts. And to stop it, to stop the hurt you have to turn it into a story. And not just a story you play over and over for yourself, but a story that you tell. A story's not a story unless you tell it. And once you tell it, it's not yours anymore. You give it away. And once you give it away it's not something that hurts you anymore, it's something that helps everyone who hears it. It's the kind of thing that is hard to explain. It's probably best if I just show you how it works.[21]

....

21   Daniel MacIvor, *How It Works*, (Winnipeg: Scirocco Drama, 2006), 13.

A story's not a story unless you tell it.

I've shared my story, and now I give it away to you. And I truly hope it helps your story.

ACKNOWLEDGEMENTS

Thank you to everyone who read my manuscript in its rough stages and expressed their enthusiasm, concerns, and helpful corrections; you bolstered me emotionally through the writing process. I'm especially grateful to Rosemary Neering, who read *Throw Another Pebble on the Pile* after a still-messy second draft. I knew you would be honest and direct with your feedback, and it was a pivotal moment for me when you said, "This work is publishable." You have been the mentor I have needed throughout this process.

Like many debut authors, I had no idea that writing a book was only half the process; I didn't realize how much work was involved in publishing it. The team at FriesenPress helped me think through each detail and made the process uncomplicated. Thank you, Kaelyn, Alyssa, Drew, and Katie.

Lastly, John: You came home from a walk and said, "You should write a book because you have something to say to women… and men need to hear it too." Thank you for your unwavering support and for being a man who believes in equality for women.

For more information about Michelle Felice
or to contact her, please visit throwanotherpebble.com.

Let's continue the conversation about women in leadership. Is your book club interested in an author visit? I'd be delighted to attend your next meeting virtually to discuss *Throw Another Pebble on the Pile*. I'd love to hear about your experiences both within and outside of the church.

9 781038 321671